TENNESSEE WILLIAMS IN BANGKOK

TENNESSEE WILLIAMS IN BANGKOK

EDDIE WOODS

inkblot 2013

ISBN 0 934301 71 9

Cover photo © 2013 by Surya Green.
The Bangkok skyline in the 1970s, as seen from the Temple of Dawn
(Wat Arun) in Thonburi, across the Chao Phraya river.

Back cover photo of Eddie Woods © 2013 by Sacha de Boer.

Photo of Eddie Woods at the Bangkok Post © 1971, 2013 by Harry Rolnick.

Photo of Tennessee Williams, 1974 © 1974, 2013 by Gerard Malanga.

Reproductions of *Sidestreet* and the original publication of
One Audience in Search of a Character are compliments of the
Bangkok Post archives.

Special thanks to Charles Henn and Philip Wagner.

Note: The photos of Eddie Woods in Bangkok survived only because
Eddie had sent prints to his mother before going to Bali, where he
eventually burned practically everything of artistic value as an act of
'spiritual renunciation.' Including photos he'd taken of Tennessee Williams.

In Memoriam: Dr. Max Henn (1906-2002)

Inkblot Publications

Distributed by aftermathbooks.com
Providence, Rhode Island

Layout & Design: millionsofimages.com
Providence, Rhode Island

Contents

For Tang Ee Liang (Kim) and Tennessee Williams,
the two key players in this journey down memory lane.
And for Theo Green, without whose encouragement
the story might never have been told.

I

Toward the end of his *Memoirs*, Tennessee Williams briefly mentions the press conference in Bangkok's Oriental Hotel (he calls it the Hotel Orient, but never mind), and how he was asked if it were true that he'd come to Bangkok to die. Though he doesn't say, it was my friend Harry Rolnick who asked him that. Harry, a copy of whose book, *A Samlor Named Desire*, Tennessee signed and inscribed for him: 'So nice meeting you in Bang Cock!' [A *samlor* is a three-wheeled bicycle rickshaw, since replaced only in Bangkok by the motorized *tuk-tuk*.] That book, now well out of print, is a collection of Harry's weekly columns in the *Bangkok Post*, the English-language newspaper we both worked on at the time. This was in 1970. After cruising the Pacific aboard the S.S. President Cleveland, and stopping off at several ports, Tennessee flew from Hong Kong to the City of Angels (the literal translation of Bangkok's abbreviated Thai name, *Krung Thep*) in early October. Which is when he and I first met, at that very press conference. The following day the *Post*'s competitor, the *Bangkok World*, ran a detailed account of the entire question and answer session.

"My," Tennessee said to me after reading it, "that girl remembered every word. It's all in there."

I smiled and replied: "Hardly. Didn't you notice her little black microphone? She was recording you."

"Oh. But at least she got it."

As for my piece on Tennessee, that's a story in itself. The features editor, Geoff, told me not to rush. To instead come up with something special, something that would put what he was sure the *World* would run to shame. So I took my time. And the more time I took, the more nervous the *Post*'s managing director (i.e., the publisher) was getting. Michael J. Gorman, an appointee of the Thomson organization, which then owned the paper. I waited a week. And in the meantime busied myself with other things. As a features writer, plus the paper's food & drink editor, I had stuff in nearly every day.

"Okay, now's good," Geoff suddenly says on day seven. "Let's have it."

"Have what?" I asked. "Tennessee Williams? I haven't even written the damn thing!"

"Well write it now, buddy. It's got to be in tomorrow's edition."

Way to go. Crunch time.

Memory fades. Had I been thinking about what I would write? Or did I make it all up on the spot? Either way, I came up with a play. 'A dialogic contrivance in three scenes' entitled *One Audience in Search of a Character*. A play I was certain I'd never see again. Until my friend Charles Henn recently went to the *Post*'s archives room and found it. (Charles is the current owner of the fabled Atlanta Hotel, about which more anon.) Then had the broadsheet-size page digitally photographed, and the photo converted to a high-resolution jpeg that he straightaway emailed to me. Not only has nothing of the *Bangkok Post* from that 'ancient era' been digitized, the archives room itself has neither a photocopy machine nor a scanner! While all the issues, a few decades' worth, are kept in big cardboard binders from which individual copies cannot be removed. So thank you, Charles. Who said in his email that he was happy to do it "for old times' sake."

The play is loosely based on the press conference and intentionally fanciful. A quasi-surreal comedy of sorts. And the final scene pure black comedy. There are three silly factual errors in the original introduction. None of which the main character seemed to mind when he later read the play. Including that his real name was Tennessee Williams. Not true. His actual name, the name on his passport, was Thomas Lanier Williams. I was well acquainted with Tennessee's work, but didn't yet know much about his life. Although that I should have known. We'd already started hanging out, and early on he told me to call him Tom. "Most of my friends do," he'd said. Still, to all intents and purposes his real first name *was* Tennessee.

I wrote the play in about an hour. With Geoff

Eddie at the *Bangkok Post* (1971).

looking over my shoulder and taking away each page to get typeset the moment it rolled off my manual Underwood, without giving me a chance to read over what I'd just written. And then coming back to wait for the next one. And the next. All of this in the *Post*'s huge editorial room. Where dozens of other people are likewise banging away at typers. Or shouting, calling for copy boys. Or talking loudly on telephones. The only staffers with their own offices (glass enclosed, so you could see them and they you!) were Nick, the managing editor; Suthichai Yoon, the city editor; and up a set of wooden stairs, overseeing us all, our distinguished Pakistani editorial director, Mr. S. M. Ali, a renowned expert on foreign affairs.

Also standing beside my desk, reading every word I'm writing, was Harry Rolnick. "Oh look, that's me," he'd exclaim. You couldn't mistake Harry, even though his name was fictionalized. As were all the names, except for Tennessee Williams. He was there under his real name!

Alas, the play doesn't end happily for its fictional author. But the day it appeared, on the front page of the Sunday Magazine, was a happy occasion for everyone. And for Mike Gorman, in particular. Having read the play in his office (which was God knows where, I never saw it), he came striding across the room with his arm outstretched and wearing an ecstatic smile.

"For a play it was well worth waiting a week!" he said, shaking my hand hard.

"Does that mean I'll be getting a raise?" I asked

Geoff after Gorman had retreated to his lair.

"Haha," Geoff replied.

Dear reader, I can hear your mind ticking away. You want to read the play, yes? Well okay, go have a peek. It's appended at the end. But bookmark this page first, so you can come back here afterward. I've only just started, there's a long way to go, and I don't want to lose you!

*

Thus begins my tale, precisely where Williams' autobiographical reminiscences start drawing to a close. Once the conference was over, Harry and I (along with Harry's housemate, Les) went up to Tennessee and asked whether he might like us to show him 'underground Bangkok,' by which we meant the gay bars.

"That would be nice," he replied, smiling broadly. "Shall we start now? I'll just go freshen up."

Harry and I were well known at the Oriental, and on especially good terms with Jürgen Voss, their food & beverage manager. (Back then the hotel's Normandie Grill was considered one of the world's best French cuisine restaurants.) Nor was Les' face unfamiliar to the hotel staff. He and Harry shared a rented house, complete with garden and a separate servants' quarters. Whereas I lived in a large, well-appointed room in the Viengtai Hotel in Banglampoo, a short walk from the newspaper's offices, near the Democracy Monument. (Later on I moved to a suite in the Trocadero Hotel on Surawong Road, as would Harry.) That's what Westerners did in Bangkok; there were no apartments, as such.

So off to the bars we went. Starting with the Tulip, followed by the Sea Hag, and wherever else. There were only a small handful. From then on it was just me and Tom, no more Harry and Les. Dinners at various restaurants, the bars for dessert. And the boys.

That stay, lasting nearly two years, was my third time in Bangkok. (A fourth occasion was in 1976, when I visited for a month.) I went by train from Singapore, thanks to Kim. And Kim is?

One of my granddaughters asked me a most interesting question a couple of years back. She was 17 then, visiting me in Amsterdam from near Munich, where she lives with her mother and two sisters. We were in my room smoking a joint.

"Tell me something, Eddie," she said. (Hannah switches back and forth from Eddie to Opa, depending on her mood. For this she was definitely in an Eddie mood.) "You've been with many women in your life, had any number of relationships, affairs, one-night stands, whatever. I'm not going to ask you who was the 'best,' that would be absurd. And you probably couldn't say, or wouldn't want to try. But what if...and this is hypothetical, yes? What if you could remember only one of your numerous lovers. Who would it be?"

"Wow," I said. "Now I know even better where all that fantastic poetry you write comes from!"

"No memory at all," Hannah repeated, "of any of

the others. Only the one. And her you'd remember clearly."

I mused on it, but not for long. And gave my answer.

"I'm going to throw you a curve ball, sweetness. You know I'm bisexual, right? Well, the one would be Kim. My Chinese drag-queen prostitute lover in Singapore. Who kept me for three months. Fed me, fucked me (and me her), saw to it that I had a roof over my head with a bed under it for us to make love on and sleep in. All of that and more. And then when she knew I wanted to go to Bangkok to land a paying job writing, gave me the money to get there. Plus sent me money afterwards, until I wrote telling her I was settled and drawing a salary. So yes, it would be Kim. Of all my lovers, she was the most unique."

"Cool," said Hannah. And took another hit off our joint.

II

I like trains. Or did when you could still smoke on them! And so had gone by train to Singapore from Bangkok, after flying there from Manila with my spy friend Carl. That time round staying at the Atlanta Hotel. Which between my efforts (handing out Atlanta business cards, with my name on the back, to every hippie I'd encounter) and those of my Indian friend Mohan—who went out to Don Muang Airport and practically dragged long-haired arriving passengers to the place!—put the Atlanta on the budget hotel map, where it has remained ever since.

"Du bekommst Geld von mir (I owe you money)," said Dr. Max Henn (Charles Henn's father, and the hotel's founding proprietor) upon my return to Bangkok compliments of Kim. And the 1000 baht (about 50 dollars US) he gave me was far from chickenfeed in 1970s Thailand.

Went down to Singapore to meet up with Carl, who'd gone on ahead of me.

"How much money do you have?" a snippy young immigrations official wanted to know at the Singapore-Malaysian border.

My reply came close to getting me turned away. Minor grief did ensue, but I managed to survive it. And from the train station made my way to Sam Leong Road, where most of the dirt-cheap hippie hotels were located. I found Carl in no time flat, at a table in the quarter's big tarp-covered outdoor café, sipping boiling hot coffee (the only way he'd drink it) from a recycled condensed milk tin. As soon as he'd finished and we'd chatted a bit, we walked to the flophouse he was checked into so I could also get a room. You paid by the day, and the moment you did it got noted on a small date card that lived on the top of the clothes cupboard. It was in these hotels and the café and along all the nearby roads that I handed out those Atlanta Hotel cards. Providentially, you might say, in light of all the shit that was about to hit the area's fan.

Carl and I were practically broke. So while trying

to figure out some kind of hustle or scam (we'd done it elsewhere, so why not here), or in a real pinch even find jobs (which in fact Carl ultimately did, one that took him to an oil rig in Sumatra), we started hocking whatever small valuables we had. The daily rent needed paying and we had to eat, however meagerly. Good fortune also occasionally came to the rescue. Like when this chap who'd been eyeing us in the café sat down at my table (I was alone at the time) and laid fifty bucks on me.

"I can tell you guys are down on your luck," he said. "But you strike me as nice fellows, and I'm sorta' flush just now. Here's my address in Australia, you can repay me if you're ever in a position to. And if not, don't worry, it'll come back to me in other ways."

Undoubtedly it did. Nor will I ever forget him and his kind gesture.

I passed the daytimes reading, strolling around (usually on my own), or sitting in the café writing this 'n that in a spiral notebook. (Notebook I no longer have. It went up in flames two years later in Bali, on the same 'spiritual renunciation pyre' that consumed more than fifteen years' worth of manuscripts and correspondence, among which the letters and cards Tennessee and I eventually exchanged, beginning with the ones he wrote me from Pattaya.) I did whatever one does in a new and interesting place and when you have no money to spend. Then late at night, having heard it talked about, I'd wander over to Bugis Street and park myself at an outdoor table nursing a single drink until close to dawn, when one of the *kai thais* would take me home with her. Outrageously exquisite transvestites of varying ethnicities: Chinese, Malay, Indian, Filipino, Indonesian, Thai... and for sure at least one Australian. I wasn't looking for it, hardly expected it, it simply started happening. And kept happening. Night after night. Every time a different sister. (That's how they referred to each other, as sisters.) Whichever of them finished turning tricks first and felt like tucking this strangely solitary lad under her wing until late morning or early afternoon. Celeste, Yvonne, Carolina, Maggie... Buy me a drink, grab us a cab to her place (where during the preceding hours she had entertained God knows how many men...unless she'd been contenting herself with giving blowjobs behind the cement latrine in the refuse lot), take me to bed. And when we arose make breakfast. Then more often than not press a few coins in my hand, for the bus fare to Sam Leong and to help me get through the day.

There's barely a resemblance between daytime Bugis Street and what it transforms into after dark. From midday till dusk it's a small bazaar selling second-hand clothing, pirated phonograph records, cheap toys and such. There are inexpensive eateries, but not yet with their nighttime stands out in front. The black Austin taxis are busy in other parts of town, and there's nary a whore in sight. Those are for the witching hour onwards. For when the ordinary sheds its disguise, comes tantalizingly alive, and the vibrations are phantasmagoric. They invade all your senses simultaneously; an ongoing barrage of bright and crude colored lights, odors sweet and pungent from the countless food stalls and the constant clashing of incongruous music, both melodious and rank. And there is never a letup. In the humid air surrounding a hundred or so outdoor tables, thick alcohol-tainted breaths mix unwarily with the strong smells of frying vegetables, fish, thin strips of succulent pork, and of course noodles. Just below the verandahs of several dilapidated restaurants, fruit sellers call out the prices of fresh juices and slices of pineapple; waiters carry huge trays stacked with steam boats and curried prawns; a cluster of merry and half-drunk Maoris sing folk songs and play guitar; and an emaciated Chinese hooker tells Charlie the British gob to go fuck himself.

On the last night I had any reason to go to Bugis Street I was down to one dollar, their kind. The shoeshine boys see my rubber sandals, my flip-flops, and leave me alone. The 10-year old tick-tack-toe hustlers know I don't want to play. For the zillionth time I'm hearing a deformed pimp scream-sing "Pagliacci" at the top of his lungs. And know if that grizzled old man with the balloons and panda bears again tries to sell me a water pistol, I may just buy one and squirt him in the face. Yet I am very much at peace. From the moment I enter this uncompromisingly sordid atmosphere I feel incredibly horny and utterly alive. I also feel as though I am going mad, which— thank the good Lord—I surely am. How else to be? Sitting with an empty glass, beholding a swish dazzle of comely trans-lovelies, watching them slink and weave alongside the tables tossing out kisses and insults with the same irresistible panache.

All at once standing in front of me is Kim. She is absolutely stunning. Even Tennessee, when he meets her months later and she is dressed to the lady-boy nines, will think so. Which is saying something, given that drag wasn't particularly Tom's cup of tea. This despite his unrestrained affection for Candy Darling, the transsexual 'Warhol superstar' who played Violet in the 1972 off-Broadway production of Williams' *Small Craft Warnings*.

"Hello."

"Hello."

"I can sit?"

"Why not?"

"Feel rich enough to buy me a beer?"

"No."

"Then I better buy you one," she says.

"Okay."

Time lapses. Casual conversation, another beer, cigarettes. And the occasional snide remark courtesy of some sailors gawking at us from nearby. There's hardly any light where Kim and I sit, the very last table at the cross-street end of the quarter. Down a ways toward the taxis, a scrawny Chinaman with his back to a fence deals blackjack on a portable card table. Only one other person plays but there are people looking on. Suddenly it is daybreak. Amongst the stragglers are neither tourists nor businessmen, and the few seamen left are obviously too pissed to move. The restaurants have pulled their stalls in from the dirt road and planked sidewalks, the food carts have been wheeled or cycled away. All the female whores split ages ago, the moonlighting bar girls. The sisters too are gone. Ah, but the Maoris are still singing like it was forever a new day. They seem an indestructible breed, eternally optimistic. Bugis Street dissolves into a warm, misty morning. Kim and I head to one of the hacks and drive off.

"Katong," she tells the driver. And a flying cockroach goes *splat* against the windshield.

"Sleep is going to feel good," says Kim.

"I'll be happy for a bed myself," I add.

"I meant that literally," she replies.

"Huh?"

"About sleeping. I meant that literally."

Her slender Chinese face smiles. Soft eyes, not young, not old. We hold hands.

Sleep does feel good...eventually. Kim undresses me, then herself. She drapes the clothing neatly over a chair. Her back is to me. Now she turns, faces the bed. She kneels, she hovers, she lies down beside me. Her smooth body is firm, tender. And her erect penis both strong and feminine. She penetrates me easily, deeply. Most unusual, this. Eddie has an exceptionally tight ass. Yet with Kim it will never hurt.

She fucks and I have a double orgasm. Narrow fingers rhythmically grip my cock, sharp painted fingernails tease my tightened balls. Now the come is spurting everywhere, Kim's tongue licking my chest, my nipples, my lips, my tongue, my eyes, my ears, lips, chest, her cock bolt hard inside of me, Kim still fucking, still beating and biting and scratching. And somewhere inside of what I think is my head, my brain, my whatever, a host of wrongheaded notions goes up in smoke and smithereens. And with it the myth that drag queens don't fuck. No doubt about it, I've died and gone to sexual heaven.

III

I did mention to Tom that I'd spent time in Singapore and had a lover there. If I'd been more specific about Kim, it might have better prepared him for the *kai thais* of Bugis Street. But how was I to know that the likes of Tennessee Williams would need preparing for anything where matters sexual were concerned? Our tastes in boys were vastly different. Tom liked them butch, or in any event decidedly masculine. I was a strange bird, and never more so than in my Bangkok years. At my most outrageous I fluttered about in effeminate unisex clothing, and flaunting all the usual super-camp body language. And yet I was almost exclusively drawn to distinctly feminine types, and drag queens in particular. Oddly enough, they were to me as well.

"What are we doing together anyway?" one of the 'girls' would frequently say, as we strolled arm-in-arm along Patpong Road or wherever. "I like men, for heaven's sake!"

"Don't sweat it, dear," I'd reply. "We're just two

lesbians having a fling."

And that's how I saw myself, how I felt sexually. I was a male lesbian. A feminine guy who dug making it with young feminine males. But who also very much enjoyed having sex with women. Bisexual androgynous, I suppose you could say. I hardly ever cross-dressed. And even though as a child I'd go to bed wishing that in the morning I would wake up a girl, it never remotely crossed my mind to have a sex-change operation.

"What do guys have that women don't?" a male friend who was finding it difficult to comprehend homosexuality once asked me. The answer was so obvious that he couldn't see it.

"A cock," I said.

So that's me. I like cunt and I like cock. By the time Tennessee and I met, he was strictly into the latter. Indeed, he'd had only one sexual experience with a woman in his life, a short but deep affair that he never regretted. She had, after all, taken his cherry. An earlier hetero romance had gone on for much longer, albeit without being consummated.

When Tom and I went out on the town, my behavior was more subdued, as was my mode of dress. So that by comparison it was his gestures and speech patterns that had an air of camp about them. The puckered lips and occasional flick of the wrist sort of thing. We'd go to a restaurant and then to a bar. And always split the dinner bill down the middle. Except for the wine. That he would pay.

"I simply must have an excellent Château

Margaux with my meal," he'd told me. "And since I know you can't afford that, the wine will always be on me." Ditto any expensive white wines, such as when we'd have fish or certain fowl. Seldom. Tom was a big red-meat eater.

The first time we visited the Tulip alone, one of my steady boyfriends was behind the bar. Dang. A common name in Thailand. I had two boyfriends named Dang. This was tall Dang.

"Tonight you are going to fuck me!" he'd sometimes insist. Knowing as he did that I was usually hot-to-trot to suck his cock and have him suck mine. Do 69. Plus I prefer fucking female asses.

"Hello," said Dang. "You're Tennessee Williams."

Tom turned and looked me dead in the eyes. His smile was piercing. That and one slightly raised eyebrow said it all. Dang caught on instantly. And without missing a beat said, "I saw your picture in the newspaper." Whew. The moment was saved, and with it a budding friendship. For yes, I had foolishly told Dang that I'd be coming that night with the great playwright. As to whether he had actually seen TW's photo in the paper, I hadn't a clue. Dang was so many things: handsome, femininely masculine, fun, a magnificent lover. And highly intelligent. God bless him.

I'd seen something approaching that look before. Also directed at me, but sans the connotation of betrayal. It was at the press conference. I'd had the temerity to call Tennessee on something he'd said which struck me as an inconsistency. To which he impishly replied, "What was it someone once said about a foolish consistency?" Yo, touché. While that someone was of course Ralph Waldo Emerson: "A foolish consistency is the hobgoblin of little minds."

Mohamed Choukri, in his book *Tennessee Williams in Tangier*, remarks on TW's "strange way" of looking at one.

"He's surely forming an opinion of me right now," the author says to himself.

We didn't spend all our after-dinner hours picking up boys in bars, mind you. Although those we did pick up, we always brought back to his suite. Or if my fancy hadn't been tickled, I'd shepherd Tom and his short-time squeeze to the hotel, say goodnight in the lobby, and take off. (I seriously doubt Tom ever went to the bars alone.) Now and then we'd order digestifs and talk. Or rather he'd mostly talk and I'd listen. Tom liked talking about his life, as opposed to discussing literary matters. While if we neither lingered nor went to the bars, he'd go his way (most likely to read or write or turn in early) and I mine. My way would often be the bars, which I regularly frequented even on the evenings between when Tom and I met up. There I'd sip Green Spot, a noncarbonated orange drink. (Other than with dinner, I rarely drank alcohol in the East. My preferred high was grass, which I was first turned on to in Hong Kong, at the 'tender age' of 29.) Or I'd go for a special massage, meaning a cursory rubdown segueing into a blowjob. Thai masseuses are adorable. Or when in the mood to create a stir, I'd scandalize the Tulip Bar by bringing a drag queen with me, a *katoy*. All these flipping queens in normal male attire—dancing, kissing, feeling one another up—and that horrified them. I loved it. On one occasion I went accompanied by a woman. No problem, the denizens of the Tulip adored her! Yeah right, go figure.

Unlike Paul Bowles' autobiography, *Without Stopping* (which according to William Burroughs, and I agree, ought to have been called 'Without Telling'!), Tennessee's *Memoirs*, published in 1976, is an open and revealing book. He had nothing to hide, not about what he'd done or what he thought. Here and there a name is changed, out of discretion or legal necessity. Other than that there's total honesty. Tennessee Williams was an honest person. Thus one omission I do find odd. He'd spoken to me about an earlier trip to the Orient. And of when sojourning in Thailand meeting and spending time with the near-legendary Jim Thompson, the 'silk king' who mysteriously disappeared in the Cameron Highlands of Malaysia in 1967 and whose body was never found. (Tom also spoke briefly of Jim at the press conference.) Naturally we speculated on what might have happened to Thompson. Everyone did. To this day they're speculating. Yet no mention is made in the *Memoirs* of this 1959 voyage. And therefore also not of the time Tennessee spent in Tokyo visiting with the celebrated Japanese author Yukio Mishima, who fired his interest in Kabuki and Noh theater. He discusses him later, but in another context.

Tom last saw Yukio during his 1970 stopover

in Yokohama. They had dinner together. Yukio was concerned about his friend's 'drinking habits,' and phoned him the next day to reiterate that. Mishima committed seppuku while Tennessee was in Bangkok, after our return from Singapore. Tom was understandably distressed, but not surprised. He said so then and he says it in the *Memoirs*. That he sensed from Yukio's demeanor when he entered the Yokohama hotel bar that something was up. There was a "tension and gravity" about him. And we now know that Mishima had meticulously planned his ritual suicide a good year in advance, indicating that the coup d'état he attempted to inspire shortly before killing himself was merely a pretext. Tom reckoned (and others have since agreed) that with the completion of the final book in his *Sea of Fertility* tetralogy, Mishima felt he had accomplished all that he needed to as an artist. He'd finished writing *The Decay of the Angel* in August 1970. It was published posthumously the following February.

Tennessee was sufficiently impressed by his 1959 interactions with Mishima, that not long afterward he began work on an 'Occidental Noh play' entitled *The Day on Which a Man Dies*. Dedicated to Mishima, it has been described as a 'fantasy-riff' on the death of the American painter Jackson Pollock, a close friend of Williams'. Kept 'in reserve' by the playwright, the manuscript was sold to a university archive in 1970, rediscovered in 1984, and first staged in its original form only in 2008. By which time theater critics were finally waking up and viewing Tennessee's experimental work more kindly, and with greater 'nous,' than had heretofore been the case. Williams' *In the Bar of a Tokyo Hotel* was a commercially-intended reworking of that Noh play.

The two men had met before, however. Tom probably told me the year, but I forget. It was in New York's Times Square and they were both cruising for sex. Tom said he picked Yukio up. Either way, introductions were put on hold until after their mutual concupiscence had been allayed. There's not a hint of this in the *Memoirs*. So am I gossiping now? Was Tom gossiping, with that and other personal tidbits he divulged to me? I guess. Gore Vidal didn't mind gossiping for my ears in 1971, including about his old friend Tennessee. One of the most all-around intelligent people I've ever met, Gore could also jokingly mimic Williams to a tee. Harold Norse, another unflinchingly honest person, didn't shy from telling in his memoirs what he'd told me years earlier, namely that his first encounter with Allen Ginsberg was when he picked the younger poet up in a New York subway car. As the American writer William Levy keenly observed, "History without gossip is a dry biscuit." I concur, providing one doesn't go overboard.

IV

Upon taking leave of the sister who had lovingly sheltered me for the night, I'd make my way to Sam

Leong Road, pay another day's rent at the hotel, and go look for Carl. To his mind I was 'bent.' But by Singapore he'd grown used to it, having already learned of my homosexual tendencies in Hong Kong. Then I met Kim and it was several days before Carl saw me again. And by the time he did, almost all the hippies were gone.

"What the hell happened?" I asked.

"There was an immigrations raid. Nearly everyone got sent packing. Most are likely in Bangkok by now, clutching those little cards you've been handing out. Dr. Henn will be over the moon. But oh shit, I gotta go to the police station. Where the fuck you been?"

"Police? What for? I met someone, I was with her. She's invited me to move in. What about the police?"

"Hey, man, I was worried. Thought you'd gotten mugged or something. I reported you missing."

"You did what! How very thoughtful. Are you nuts? Go straighten it out, quick! Here's where I'll be," I said, jotting down the Katong address and handing it to him. "But don't tell the cops. Say you were mistaken, I'm safe, I went to Thailand. Say anything. Go!"

He did, and I headed back to Kim's. As well as taking me in, without either of us knowing it she'd saved me from getting busted and possibly deported. Carl looked too straight to get deported. And had they tried, he'd have switched to his best British accent (he was half English, half American) and laid one of his more condescending upper middle-class raps on them.

And so began an incredible three-month love affair. Me and Tang Ee Liang, the forever unforgettable Kim. The apartment she lived in was up one flight of stairs and spacious. About half a dozen sisters shared it, each with their own room. Plus there were two toilets, a washroom with a shower, and a sizeable kitchen. And a fat, jovial amah who arrived bright and early every morning and stayed till early evening; cooking, washing clothes, ironing, keeping the flat clean, doing other chores and running errands. Throughout the day you'd hear her being called to in one high-pitched voice or another: "Ai-eee! Ai-eee!" All the sisters, with the single exception of Kim, were terribly high-strung and constantly in need of attention. Aiee provided much of that. And in time so did I, by sitting, listening, and occasionally giving advice.

The raid had been in the papers. One of the sisters gave the previous day's *Straits Times* to Kim and she showed it to me when I returned from what proved to be a narrow escape from the law. They'd planned it for a while. Part of the government's never-ending cleanup campaign. Public spitting was already banned; uniformed monitors were instructing commuters how to queue for busses in an orderly manner; 'unsightly' neighborhoods were slowly being razed (not so much on account of the buildings, rather the inhabitants!). And soon foreigners flying to Singapore whose hair was deemed unacceptably long would have their locks cut at the airport before being granted entry. Hippies already in the country had to go. Their outlandish apparel, along with the dope-smoking and other 'antisocial' conduct (Singapore had then, and still has, among the harshest drug laws of any nation on the planet), was seen as setting a bad example for the tiny republic's youth. Next in line would be Bugis Street. Singapore's three primary attributes are money, law & order, and image. And the last of those in terms of how they view themselves, not how others see them.

In many ways living in the Katong apartment resembled featuring in an Andy Warhol movie. I'm New York neurotic, but my neuroses couldn't hold a candle to what the sisters relentlessly displayed. Again apart from Kim, one or more were continually on the verge of a nervous breakdown. And of course they were all drama queens. They got high on their theatrics. If I'd had a film camera I could have made my own psychedelic version of a Warhol flick. No directing required, just keep shooting. Which is what I did. With my eyes and my mind. The canisters are stored in my memory bank.

During the day Kim and I were almost always in one another's company. When the weather was clement, we'd go out and she'd show me the city. Every nook and cranny of it. We'd walk or take busses. We'd stop at food stalls and she'd introduce me to a variety of Singaporean delicacies. She dressed as a boy then, loose-fitting shirt and trousers. And no makeup. Drag was for when she was working, or rare special occasions (such as our eventual double dinner date with Tennessee and Amanda). Whereas the rest of the sisters pretty much stuck to female garb, even at home. Although Kim too would slip into a nighty come evening, and also wear it at breakfast. Otherwise we passed long hours in her room, now our room. We'd smoke marijuana, slim joints rolled with powerful Aceh (northern Sumatra) weed that Kim knew where to score safely. (It came in tan paper cylinders called *katoos*.) And listen to music. Kim had an amazing collection of LP's and 45's. I'd missed the Sixties musically (I was 'elsewhere,' doing other things); only caught up with that scene from the Seventies on. And it all started with Kim: Jimi Hendrix, the Rolling Stones, *Abbey Road*... An education that would continue in Bangkok, when I was writing album reviews for the *Post* and had my own radio program, with free access to Radio Thailand's enormous record library. Plus we read. I joined a local library and kept checking out books. *Moby Dick* was one of them. First I read it and then Kim did. And while she was reading it I was at the library doing research on whales!

Nor did a day or night go by without our having sex. Lots of it. I've already described some of what transpired the first time we slept together. No need to embellish further. Other than to say it was out-of-sight remarkable. All the more so because we were in love. In love and the sisters loved that we were. They were a family, and I was part of it.

For sure there were days when I had a yen for relative solitude and went for long walks on my

25

own. Or Kim had matters to attend to, which were best done minus me tagging along. One sweltering hot afternoon I walked the entire length of Orchard Road (just under a mile and a half), a seemingly endless poem reeling itself off in my mind. It was like listening to a poetry reading on the radio. I was enthralled. I did have some paper and a pen with me. But couldn't bring myself to stop and write any of it down, for fear that the flow of words I was hearing would cease. Yet vaguely wishing a taping gizmo were attached to my brain and recording it. All of a sudden I was at the top of the road and the end of the poem. I sat on a bench or a low wall, pulled paper and pen from my cloth shoulder bag, and...couldn't recall a single line! Nada. Okay, maybe it wouldn't have been on a par with Coleridge's incomplete masterpiece, "Kubla Khan." But it was good, I knew for certain that what I'd heard was good. And now it had vanished. There was nothing for it but to laugh out loud, wander home, and tell Kim. Kim who smiled, who kissed me, and then took me to bed.

And Kim who'd now begun working less and less. For one, she didn't feel to. She liked being with me at night, not sucking strange dicks or having alien cocks rammed up her ass. An ass many of those who fucked her thought was a cunt. The bloke's more than a trifle tipsy. He's been propositioned by a sister who is looking every inch female. The lights are off when they undress, lie down, and she inserts his tool where it has to go, usually from behind. Yet Kim didn't have girl tits. She wasn't interested. She was

26

a boy queer who dug cross-dressing, for fun and the bucks she could earn with it. Some of the sisters were getting hormone shots, and thinking about having the op. Meanwhile their boobs could be grabbed and fondled, adding to the illusion. Kim had ways of keeping her johns from fondling her.

"Let's get right to the fucking," she'd say. "That's what I want, to get fucked." And taking hold of his cock add: "You too, isn't it? Or would you rather I suck you and you shoot your whole load in my mouth?"

Equally important, Kim sensed my growing uneasiness. Not jealousy exactly. It wasn't like she was 'seeing' someone else. Possessiveness? On the edge of, would be fair to say. Oh hell, I simply wasn't comfortable with other guys screwing her, is all. And she wasn't comfortable with me being uncomfortable. But we couldn't live on air, and the money had to come from somewhere. When she did work, she either had to take her john to a hotel or use another sister's room. I'd be asleep in ours, right? (I told her just do it, I understand, I'll be fine. Then I'd watch her dress. From her shoes and net stockings to one of her marvelous wigs. Wow, she was so fucking beautiful!) Could I really sleep when Kim was working? Yes and no. What I didn't hear I could live with. Yet let the key turn in the front door lock and I'd be instantly awake. One night it turned with a vengeance and a whole noisy crowd came bursting in. Three or four sisters and an equal number of tricks. Among whom Kim, her voice was unmistakable. So was Amanda's—deep-throated, sensuous. They were about to have a party. With the doors to whichever rooms they were using wide open. The guys had brought booze with them. They drank and they fucked. The sisters pretended to drink, between sucking cocks and getting buggered. And deftly rolling each and every one of the fuckers. Before waving goodbye to them as they stumbled down the stairs,

"Go right, then left, walk a ways and you'll find a taxi stand. See you! Kiss, kiss!!"

Oh, no worries, they'd left them enough pocket change for that. And what a cacophony of glee ensued once the suckers were on their way, clueless to even what part of town they were in.

"Ladies, look. So much money! I've always said go for business types. They're loaded. And such children. It's like taking candy from, as they say. Sailors are pains, no? And cheapskates."

It was definitely Amanda speaking. Then the others joined in. Blah-blah-blah. Though not Kim. Her silence was ear-splitting. She stayed till their takings were counted. Amanda would hold onto it overnight, they'd divvy up in the morning. After which everyone went to bed. Kim had made herself ready for that before coming to our room and crawling in with me. And holding me tight. Good God did I ever love her!

The household didn't often do breakfast or lunch together, only sometimes dinner. But the next afternoon did find us all gathered round the kitchen table. I was uncustomarily silent.

"Cat got your tongue?" Amanda asked.

"No, just thinking."

"About what? We disturbed you last night? Kept you awake?"

"The awake part didn't bother me," I replied somberly.

"Oh? What then?"

"You robbed those guys. Stole their money. And laughed about it."

Amanda picked up a skewer of satay, pulled a chunk of meat off with her teeth, and began chewing. Staring straight at me, she pointed with an upturned hand at the assortment of dishes that Aiee was still adding to.

"Good food?" she said. Then withdrawing her hand and continuing to chew: "Kim's bed is comfortable?"

With which she looked away, yanked another piece of beef or mutton from the satay stick, and started chatting with one of the sisters. Kim, who was sitting beside me, placed a hand on my thigh and gently squeezed. My cheeks felt flushed, my armpits were sweating, but Kim's squeeze calmed the chill that had run up my spine. I took a deep breath and reached for Amanda's shoulder. She turned back towards me.

"Thank you," I said. Anything more would have diluted my apology.

Amanda smiled.

"Have some satay," she said. "Aiee's is the best, lah."

*

The sisters didn't have pimps, they were far too independent-minded for that. What Kim did have, however, for in emergencies, was a money lender-cum-pawn broker. And the less she worked, the more frequently she went to see him.

"What are you going to do, Eddie?" Tessa asked me.

Kim had gone out and we were having one of our chat sessions in the kitchen. Normally we talked about her. Her abused childhood in Manila; working there as a prostitute before coming to Singapore; the college correspondence courses she was taking. And her indecisiveness about whether to go all the way and have the op. The hormone shots had given her a cute set of petit tits, perfectly suited to her slender frame. Her appearance was at once boyish and thoroughly female.

"I know Kim's broke," she continued. "She's not keen on working, she's running out of things to hock, and she's in debt to Lee Chan up to her eyeballs."

"I've told her it's okay if she works," I said. "I can handle it."

"You say you can. But we both know that's a lie. Besides, she doesn't want you to handle it. She wants to be with you."

"Yeah. It's a bit of a bind, all right."

Then Kim came in.

"You two had lunch? No, eh. Let's get some *mee hoon*. My treat."

30

Lee Chan had obviously coughed up. As to how much deeper in the red he'd let Kim go was anyone's guess. Circumstances were dire. A bull had to be taken by the horns. And it was up to me to do the taking.

In all my years away from the States, and no matter how skint, one thing I'd not ever done was 'call home' asking for bread. Home. America had stopped being that long before I'd left her shores at age 20. No country was or would be. Yes, I'm an American writer. I was born and raised there and I love the language. Yes, I've traveled around the USA and embraced its manifold beauties. Yes, I carry an American passport. But that's where it ends. Basho said it all: "Every day is a journey, and the journey itself is home." Amen.

Yet this wasn't the time for philosophizing. It was a time for action. And so I swallowed my pride, bit the bullet, and made the dreaded call. Three calls, in fact. From a telecommunications center.

"Are you sure you want to do this?" Kim asked when we got there. "I know it goes against all your..."

"All my what? Principles? I don't have any principles, I have standards. But fuck them, too. This is reality. And more importantly, this is you. You've done so much, now it's my turn."

I phoned my sister first, but she wouldn't take the call. Told me years later she'd guessed why I was phoning, was in no position to help, but couldn't bear to refuse. Fair enough. So I tried my father. No answer. It was a Sunday, he must have gone for a drive with whatever wife he was on by then (I think the fifth). More's the pity, Dad would have sent something. That left Mother. 'Dammit,' I thought. And gave the operator the number. Lucky for me she was out visiting a sick friend. Her husband answered and unhesitatingly accepted the charges.

"What's up, kid?"

I cut straight to the chase, no elaborations.

"I'm in a jam, Phil. As much as I hate to ask, I need some money. Any chance?"

"How much, Edward?"

"Whatever you can spare. At least a hundred, if possible."

"I'll check the account and see if I can't do more. Where should I send it?"

I told him. Then added: "Oh, Phil..."

"Yes?"

"I've no idea when I can pay you back."

"Don't worry about it. Take care of yourself."

"You too, Phil. Thanks so much. Really. Give my love to Mother."

"Will do. Bye, kid."

Phil sent three hundred. A goodly sum in those days. And in Singapore very good. I gave it all to Kim. Suggesting that for starters she lay a healthy slice of it on Lee Chan. And stash the rest. Which she did.

Had Mother been there and taken the call, I would've come up empty-handed. She made sure to tell me that the last time I saw her, in 1976. Difficult relationship, exceedingly complex. Suffice it to say that we made our peace well before she died in 1987. Another amen.

I'd also been writing a lot. Mainly on the second-hand typewriter Kim bought for me soon after I moved in. Poems, stories, essays. Kim liked them, and encouraged me to keep at it.

"You're a good writer," she said. "Never stop."

It's what I'd mostly wanted since my teens. To write. But now I wanted something else, as well. Not to replace my creative writing, but to complement it. I wanted to write for money. And knew the ticket to that was journalism. So I knocked off a few sample news stories and went to see *Time* magazine's Singapore bureau chief, in hopes he would take me on as a stringer.

My samples made a positive impression. But didn't get me any work.

"I have too many stringers as it is," he said. "I could add you to the stable, but it'd be a waste. I do have a tip for you, though."

"I'm all ears," I said.

"I've heard that they're looking for a features writer on the *Bangkok World*. Here's the editor's name," he said, noting it on a slip of paper. "You can say I sent you."

"Hmm, sounds interesting. I kinda' had my heart set on staying here, but I'll definitely think it over. Much obliged."

"Don't think too long. Jobs like that get snapped up quickly."

We shook hands, he wished me luck, and I went

home to discuss what he'd proposed with Kim.

"Do it, Eddie," she said. "I'll miss you like crazy, I don't want you to go, but you should do it. It's a great opportunity. We'll check on the train times first thing tomorrow and make a reservation. I'll pay the fare. Now let's spend a beautiful night in each other's arms!"

We did just that. And so much more. But even after making ourselves ready, had to wait a while before getting to it. There was a knock at the door. It was Carl. Who wasn't in the least bit fazed when Kim answered in her nighty. He'd stopped by to say he was off to Sumatra, the oil rig gig. Said he'd write. I said address it c/o Poste Restante, Bangkok and told him why. Kim made a pot of tea, we each had a cup, and he left. It would be over a year till I saw him again. In due course I was wishing to God I hadn't!

Three months Kim and I had been together, with never once coming close to exchanging a cross word. And now we were parting. Kim booked me a 2nd-class sleeper for the two-day ride and saw me off at the station with hugs and kisses and a few tears in both our eyes. I'd said my farewells to all the sisters before leaving the flat, likewise with hugs and kisses.

Amanda: "I expect to see you again, Eddie. I'm not kidding, lah!"

She did. Twice. The second time in company with Tennessee.

There were stops along the way. Kuala Lumpur and Penang were the longest. I didn't go into town for either. My sights were set on Bangkok.

V

I went directly from Hua Lamphong Station to the Atlanta Hotel. The small amount of traveling cash I'd let Kim give me was all but gone by then, hence Dr. Henn's baksheesh was more than welcome.

"Now we have to try and find you a room. Thanks to you we're full up. But ach, the place stinks of marijuana!"

Wherever the *Time* chap had got his info, it was wrong. The *Bangkok World* was in no need of additional staff. The friendly editor suggested I try the *Bangkok Post*, and told me I should see Geoff, their features editor. An Englishman in his late twenties, Geoff was even friendlier.

"Yeah, I can use another writer. You any good?"

"I reckon so," I replied.

"We'll have to clear it with Nick first," he said. "If he agrees, you'll go and get grilled by Mr. Ali."

"Mr. Ali?"

"Mr. Ali."

The meeting with Nick took less than five minutes. I was with Mr. Ali for half an hour. He was polite but firmly focused. And wanting to know everything about me that pertained to my journalistic abilities. I lied through my teeth concerning my previous newspaper experience. I didn't have any, but said I'd worked on the *Adirondack Daily Enterprise* in Saranac Lake, New York (where I had lived for a spell, in my junior year of high school!), contributed freelance articles to the *New York Post* (they'd once published an op-ed letter of mine extolling the virtues of the Catholic Worker Movement), and whatever other impressive bullshit I could think of that he had no way of checking. He asked how I was with research, if I was good with people and could do interviews, whether I felt capable of writing in-depth social and political profiles; et cetera and so forth. That was the grilling part. I responded in the affirmative to everything he threw at me. Without mentally pausing to wonder where all this self-assurance was coming from. I passed with flying colors. Strangely enough, he never inquired about my formal education. Which was just as well. Apart from a smattering of university courses, I didn't have any after high school. I was and am an autodidact.

"And?" said Geoff when I came back down from Mr. Ali's office.

"He said I'm hired."

"Excellent. Now let's find out if you really can write. And how fast. Here's your first story," he said, handing me the address of a new shopping mall that needed covering. "Four hundred words will do. Have it on my desk in two hours. Oh, and this is your desk and typewriter."

We were standing right by it. The sports desk was behind me. Noisy. The editor, a good-natured Ceylonese fellow, seemed to be constantly on the phone. I took off. An hour and a half later Geoff had his story. I'd done it. I was getting paid to write!

Dr. Henn hadn't been putting me on. There

were no rooms available. But by cannily shifting some of the other guests around ("You move in with him!" "You, go sleep in the dormitory room, 10% discount!"...), he readily found me a suitable single on the uppermost floor. Daryl, a young American, was in one of the adjacent rooms. Mohan ('Calcutta Mo') was in another. The three of us soon became friends. Every evening after I'd knocked off work, we would walk to the top of Soi Song (Soi 2), turn the corner onto Sukhumvit Road, and park our butts at Mama's for yet another *khao pad* (fried rice) supper, that being the cheapest dish on the menu. Kim had sent me fifty dollars shortly after I'd arrived, I was now pulling in a weekly paycheck, the good doctor was giving me a cut rate on the room; but I still had to watch my pennies. Then one day Geoff dropped a godsend in my lap.

"Know anything about food?" he asked.

"I used to be a short-order cook. And I managed a steak house in Hong Kong. Plus I like to eat. Why?"

"Harry wants to stop as food & drink editor. He suggests you for it. Interested?"

"In a flash! What's it entail?"

"Talk to Harry. He'll fill you in and show you the ropes."

Unlike with some papers, where you go incognito, pay the tab and later get reimbursed, the *Post*'s policy was that you told the restaurant in advance you were coming. Made it trickier to properly evaluate them, since they'd be sure to treat you like a king. I soon got the hang of it, though. Even whilst paying close 'taste attention' to my meal, I'd observe the other tables like a hawk. The service, the customers' reactions to what they were eating. And every so often I'd ask to see the kitchen.

My first restaurant was Viennese. It'd been ages since I'd last sat down to a proper Western meal. Pure pleasure, from the dry vodka martini aperitif to the cognac and coffee. Yet it was the coffee that saw me beckon not the maitre d' but the manager to my table.

"Is something wrong, sir?"

"Everything was perfect," I replied. "There's just one thing I'm curious about."

"And that is?"

"After such a splendid meal and all, how come you serve instant coffee? It's good instant, mind. I assume freeze-dried. But instant nonetheless. When you're a coffee lover, and drink it black with no sugar, you can always tell."

"Instant coffee? No, can't be."

He went and got a cup, poured himself a small measure from the silver pot, and took a sip. He was horrified.

"I'll be right back, sir," he said, and went dashing to the kitchen, pot in hand. When he returned a few minutes later he was holding a different pot and another cup.

"My sincere apologies, sir. That should never have happened. One of the chef's assistants made a mistake. I'm not even sure where the instant coffee came from, but it's gone now. Here," he said, filling my new cup, "this is real coffee, freshly brewed. I'm truly sorry."

"It's okay," I said. "My lips are sealed."

And they were. I intentionally omitted what I decided to take for an unfortunate fluke from my review. Doing so sat well with an amusing thought I had while writing it: 'Mama's *khao pad* is all right, but who needs it!'

I still did, though not for much longer. A couple of weeks on and I was ensconced in the Viengtai. Near to which was a wonderful Thai restaurant that served a wide array of food at reasonable prices. Most of it the kind of spicy hot I adore. I lunched there almost every day. For dinner when I had to pay I experimented, mainly Thai and Chinese. I was on a roll. Diverse feature stories, interviews, the restaurant reviews and updating the monthly guide; even the occasional editorial, when no one else could be found to write it. And in the evening chill out with a joint of Buddha grass mixed with a sprinkling of tobacco. Then the bars or a boy lover who'd come round. Plus penning poems. And writing to Kim.

In the main my reviews were favorable. Yet if a restaurant needed a scolding, I'd give them one. By and large they were accepting and took heed. One owner did complain, to the advertising director. Said unless I changed my negative assessment in the monthly guide, he'd cancel his ad contract. The director demanded I do so, the contract was worth too much money. I said like hell I will. The director went to editor Nick. Nick backed me up; my write-up stayed the way it was. Editorial integrity had prevailed, even for a capsule critique of an eatery. And, the owner didn't cancel after all!

One restaurant I never had to inform in advance was the Normandie Grill. That because they were forever inviting me. Lunch, dinner, social events they were hosting. Which soon prompted me to make clear to Jürgen Voss that he shouldn't expect a review every time, that would be over the top.

"Oh no, we just like having you. When there's something special to write about, I'm sure you will. And it won't be anything like what we'd get from Friar Tuck!"

That was the pseudonym used by the *Bangkok World*'s reviewer. Whose greatest sin, as Jürgen saw it, was to insist on being served a glass of Coca Cola with his wine. I found his reviews dull, picayune. So no, Tuck wasn't someone to whom they'd send a big cake on a holiday, as they did me. It would just be there on my desk when I arrived of a morning, with a note attached: 'Love from the Normandie!'

This also had to do with being homosexual. So many Western restaurant owners, managers, and maitre d's in Bangkok were. It was a gay-friendly city, at a time when most gay European and American professional people felt unable to come out of the closet at home. In Bangkok they could relax, be themselves. Openly. The owner of a certain hotel in Pattaya was very gay. They had three restaurants and he wanted me to review them all. Invited me for a long weekend so that I could.

At the Oriental Hotel discussing an upcoming dog show, in which all were to be judges. Left to right: Unknown, Jürgen Voss (hotel food & beverage manager), Jim Davison (radio presenter), Eddie Woods, Harry Rolnick, two 'high-profile' expatriate ladies. The sculpture seen in the background is made entirely of butter!

"May I bring a friend?" I asked over the phone. "A Thai boy."

"By all means do!" he replied.

I brought tall Dang with me. They accommodated us in a spectacular suite with a triple-sized bed. And what a time Dang had. Lounging by the pool ordering drinks. Signing the tab and saying he was with Mr. Woods. Accompanying me to the restaurants. Where he wasn't too shy to pass his own judgments on the food! And after that...well, you know. As said, Dang was terrific in bed.

The story I got the biggest kick out of writing opened with the line, "There's a crummy little bar down near Patpong..." It was about a dump the likes of which I'd not seen before, despite my four years in the Air Force and a still longer stint flogging cyc's (encyclopedias) to American military personnel. A servicemen's watering hole, run by US Army Special Forces vets, catering primarily to GIs on R&R from Vietnam. And 100% gung-ho for the war. There were American flags, Confederate flags, combat photos, and all sorts of insignia; bayonets, knives and replica guns were secured to the wall behind the bar. Only John Wayne was missing, but not his likeness, which glared at you from a film poster for *The Green Berets*. Nothing other than country music blared from the jukebox; rock 'n roll was noticeably non grata. Hey, I dig country & western, and know where Merle Haggard was coming from with "Okie from Muskogee." But you can bet your boots that had the Dixie Chicks been around then, you wouldn't have heard their voices, their nitty-gritty lyrics, mingling with all the jingoistic he-man chattering. Furthermore, there were hardly any girls. This was a man's bar, where guys came to drink and shoot the shit. They could look for pussy elsewhere.

My piece didn't pull any punches. I took my cue from Brooklyn's baseball umpires, who were famously fond of saying, "I calls 'em the way I sees 'em." After it ran, Geoff said he was intrigued, he'd like to see the joint for himself, let's go there together sometime. A few days later we did. Sat at a table next to a wooden column and ordered two beers. I felt even more out of place than when I'd gone alone. Everyone seemed to be eyeing us.

"Look," said Geoff, pointing at something tacked to the column.

I looked. It was a newspaper clipping. It was my story!

We slowly finished our drinks, settled the bill, and got up. Barry Sadler's god-awful "Ballad of the Green Beret" was playing as we were leaving. But not so loudly that we couldn't hear the bartender calling after us, "Gonna write another crummy little story?"

There wasn't an inkling of crumbs in my pet restaurant review. Chokchai wins the blue ribbon for that, hands down. Not Chokchai Steak House, but the much lesser known (other than to aficionados of upcountry eats) Chokchai in the old city of Thonburi, across the Chao Phraya river. I took a coterie of culinary daredevils with me. Before the aperitif could be served, I had to go to the kitchen and select the host.

"Pick a cage, sir. If you don't like that bat, we'll try another."

There were dozens of cages. Black metal, with tiny holes to let air in. I pointed to one at random. Out came a bat. As bats go, it looked fine to me. And so with a nod I signed its death warrant. 'Forgive me, Father. Forgive me, Buddha. Forgive me, dear bat.' Much later on, in Bali and Ceylon, I came to like and appreciate bats a lot. Winged guardians of the night. Alas, this sentinel's surveillance days were done the second it got captured. Two kitchen hands held the creature by its wings while another slit the hapless mammal's throat, letting the blood trickle into a porcelain pitcher. Then rice wine was added, the mixture stirred and poured into small tumblers that were brought to our table by a waiter. We all clinked glasses in unison and drank up.

"What a surprisingly delicate libation," said Harry Rolnick.

"I'll stick to beer," his friend Les replied. "I wonder what's next."

The bat was next. First it was shown to us, skinned. Then taken away for roasting. And brought back on a large salver, nicely sliced in easy to manage pieces. It tasted like chicken. Not so what followed on. Tiger salad, chilled elephant knuckle, braised python and other snakes. An unforgettably delectable spread. *Chok* means luck, *chai* is victory. Yet when the syllables are joined, no one thinks of that. It just sounds so positive!

*

A little over a month before Tennessee waltzed into my life, I learned why Mr. Ali had so insistently queried me about writing socio-political profiles. On August 9th 1965 Singapore was expelled from the Federation of Malaysia and immediately became an independent nation. With the fifth anniversary of that momentous event looming, Mr. Ali wanted me to spend a week there gathering material for a special supplement that I would then come back and write. He supplied me with names and telephone numbers of people to interview, including the foreign minister, S. Rajaratnam, a close friend of his. Also David Marshall, a prominent opposition figure. And sundry other contacts. I was to fly down the following day. My hotel had been booked. Expenses would be fully paid. A signed note to the accounts department filled my wallet with spending money. I sent an express telegram to Kim, giving her the hotel phone number and saying she should ring me late the next day. Then hotfooted it to the Viengtai and started packing.

No sooner in Singapore, I arranged for Kim to sleep in my room. A twenty-dollar tip to the concierge guaranteed us a double bed. We made the most of our shared time. Amanda came by one evening and joined us for dinner.

"I knew I'd see you again!" she said, throwing her arms around me.

Kim didn't know. She'd been hoping, but

couldn't help wondering whether the last time we'd made love was our final curtain call.

"I really have missed you," she said after we'd crawled into bed.

"And I you," I replied.

We held one another tight, kissed long and deep, and proceeded to make the weeks between then and now disappear.

My days began early and went on uninterrupted for hours. In lieu of lunch I grabbed snacks on the go. I took copious notes, and once back at the hotel typed them up on the portable I'd brought with me. Only after that would Kim and I head for the dining room and a relaxing repast. While I was gone she'd either amuse herself reading and listening to the radio, or go for walks or to Katong to fetch another change of clothing. I'd instructed the desk clerks to give 'Miss Tang' the key whenever she asked for it. To keep their minds at ease, Kim made a point of attiring herself in casual drag. Dark feminine slacks. A lady's blouse or wide-collared shirt with a loosely-knotted necktie. And the least flamboyant of her wigs: the hair long, straight, pitch black, and with bangs. If anything she looked like a young girl playing at trying to dress as a boy!

My first port of call was the foreign ministry. A secretary escorted me into Rajaratnam's office, seated me at a small table where tea and cakes had already been set for two, and said the minister would be with me shortly. A minute or so later he was. We shook hands.

"I bring you greetings from Mr. Ali," I said.

"Yes, yes, he phoned to say you were coming. Please," he said, gesturing to the cakes and then pouring tea into both our cups. "You can help yourself to sugar or milk if you like. And now fire away. This is good timing. My next appointment is not for another...(he glanced at his watch)...well, I have time."

And so I fired. He answered every question without hesitation. A nominally Hindu Tamil (born in Ceylon, but raised in Singapore), Rajaratnam was also a former journalist whose "I write as I please" column in the *Straits Times* had never failed to incur the wrath of the British colonial government. Fiercely Singaporean, he'd co-founded (along with Lee Kuan Yew and others) the now unassailably dominant People's Action Party. And was at one with all its governing policies. He, like the prime minister, sincerely believed that for a fledgling democracy, especially of Singapore's size, a de facto one-party system was the only way to go. A vexatious opposition could often prove "inconvenient and irritating." We discussed this at length. He presented a strong case, but I wasn't convinced, and told him so. He smiled. A smile that seemed to say, 'Good thing you're not in charge here.' I also told him that I'd be seeing David Marshall.

"Oh, that will be fun!" he said, smiling much more broadly. "And perfectly correct. You want your article to be balanced. For that you need to hear more views than just mine. You'll certainly get those from David."

I asked him about the hippie evictions, the deportations. Said I was in Singapore then (but not where in Singapore, or why).

"Not my department," he responded. "But naturally I was in favor. It's not the people, per se; it's the image. We're a young country. Attracting foreign investment is vital. Harboring a hippie ghetto would hardly be conducive to that. Don't you agree?"

I nodded noncommittally. And scribbled a note to myself to omit the topic from the supplement and write a separate article on 'Singapore and the hippies' for the newspaper proper.

The intercom phone on the minister's desk buzzed. Rajaratnam went and picked up.

"Yes, of course I'm free," he told his secretary.

And turning to me said, "Lucky you."

In strode the prime minister, Mr. Lee Kuan Yew. Rajaratnam introduced us, more hand shaking, the two men held a brief conversation out of my hearing, the prime minister left.

"That was unexpected," I said. "A formidable individual, from everything I've heard and read. Though I did find the tearful anguish he unabashedly expressed over the split with Malaysia more than a little moving." Then added something to the effect of Singapore being perhaps the only country to gain independence against its will.

"That's a good line," Rajaratnam rejoined. "You should use it in your piece."

'Ever the journalist,' I thought.

Before I left, the minister made two or three phone calls on my behalf, connecting me with other people I should see. My days were getting busier.

He walked me to the office door and opened it.

"My greetings to Mr. Ali," he said, clasping my right hand in both of his. "I'll be looking forward to your story."

David Marshall was charming, witty, and refreshingly forthright. And possessed a fascinating background. A Singapore-born Orthodox Jew, he was descended from Indian Baghdadis, university educated in England, and eventually acquired repute as the colony's most successful criminal lawyer. His acquittal record in murder cases he'd defended was said to be 99%. When in 1969 Lee Kuan Yew abolished jury trials, he used Marshall as an example of the system's 'inadequacy.' Politically left-wing (he was the founder of the Workers' Party of Singapore), he'd also served briefly as First Chief Minister under the colonial government.

The interview took place in the garden of his seaside home in Changi. His input was priceless. And his love of people, and respect for the value of human life, unquestionably genuine. (This also comes through in subsequent interviews with him that I've read.) He abhorred the death penalty, and felt that every life he'd deprived the gallows from taking was a life worth saving, regardless of the crime committed. As a lifelong opponent of capital punishment, this was stirring music to my ears. Alack, the prime minister was not singing from the same hymn sheet as we were. No one in the Singapore government was. Marshall further deplored what he saw as the ever-increasing adoration of money, of accumulating wealth, the 'perverse desire' to live surrounded by material luxury. He loved Singapore, too (and in time would serve as its ambassador to four separate countries), only not the road Lee Kuan Yew was leading it along. His incisive bons mots filled an entire page in my notebook. Which is what I was using, not a tape recorder.

It was the harbor and a string of industrial complexes that I additionally wrote about (a developing nation's pride and joy). But it's the lovely lady from public relations whose image remains imbedded in my recall. She who graciously led me on a personal guided tour, and sprang for lunch (or rather her expense account did). An executive canteen in some factory or other. In the end they all look the same.

"You smell of woman," said Kim when I got back to the hotel.

"Must be her perfume," I replied nonchalantly.

"Not perfume. Woman. I may be queer, but I do know the difference."

"Should we eat downstairs or go out? I've the morning free, I can type up my notes then. I'll go take a shower now. I feel sweaty."

Kim: "And wash off her scent, is it?"

Eddie: "Hey! Ships and smokestacks. I told you before I left. A private escort courtesy of government PR. What's with you anyway?"

Kim: "Was she attractive?"

Eddie: "Very."

Kim: "Would you have liked to fuck her?"

Eddie: "In any other circumstances, yes."

Kim: "So why didn't you try? And please don't say you only have eyes for me."

Eddie: "I won't. But here and now you're the only piece of ass my loins are aching for."

Kim: "Shut up and fuck me! Then go take your shower. No, we will."

"This was beyond my wildest dreams," Kim said the day I left. "I'll be praying for a repeat. Do you think...?"

Since I had no way of knowing, I answered with a gentle kiss on her forehead. Thanks to good fortune, my visit with Tennessee in tow would not be long in coming. The last ever time I saw Kim was much later. And very different, I'm afraid.

I was given free rein on what to write. I drew parallels with Plato's *Republic* and the city-states of ancient Greece, gave credit where I felt it was due, but allowed myself to criticize. Mr. Ali was pleased with the result. As were Nick and Mike Gorman. Regarding the supplement, they were the triumvirate that counted. The sole objection (vehemently expressed, according to Geoff) came from the Singapore embassy. And had nothing to do with me. The folks in layout, the designers, hit upon the bright idea to grace the cover with a full-color photo illustration of a Chinese New Year celebration parade. A portrayal that ran diametrically counter to the integrated multiculturalism the Singapore government was doing its damndest to promote. In sooth, this core ideological divergence was the driving force behind Singapore's expulsion from Malaysia. The Singaporean factions had wanted to build a society in which all citizens, whatever their race or ethnic origins, were afforded equal rights. As opposed to what the Federation's political heavyweights believed in and ultimately got: *Bumiputra* ('son of the soil'), Malays come first. What's more, Lee Kuan Yew (born Harry Lee Kuan Yew), whose native tongue was English, didn't start learning Chinese until he was 32, a mere 10 years before becoming Singapore's prime minister. Still, it was a handsome cover. One that the embassy had no choice but to live with. And it accurately reflected reality, seeing as how the country's population was (and still is) overwhelmingly Chinese.

*

I never took Tennessee with me when reviewing a restaurant. He was inclined to dine European (where he'd have no trouble scoring his beloved Château Margaux!). And since that's what we did together, I tended toward non-Western cuisine even for reviews during the time we were hanging out. And what if he hadn't liked something? I couldn't put in my review that I was there with Tennessee Williams and he thought the salad was rubbish! Especially after he'd maybe given the manager his autograph. Ho-ho.

Tom's favorite gay bar was the Eden. All the boys were macho, and on the rough trade side of things. Nothing for me. And you couldn't just pick them up, either. You had to buy them out of the bar. And once you had them out, negotiate separately for whatever sexual favors you had in mind. That money went into their pocket, the 'bar fine' to the owner. Meaning he wasn't exactly a pimp, but more of a male madam.

"If you want my business," I said to him of an evening, "you'll need to have at least one *katoy* here. If she's a looker, I'll go for it."

"I'll do it," he said. "For you I'll do it. And let you know when."

How he proposed to let me know was left unsaid. Other than with Tom, I seldom patronized the Eden. But the fucker actually came through. Bumped into him on the street one day.

"Tonight," he said. "I'll have your ladyboy for you tonight. You come?"

I went, I saw, she conquered, and I paid. And back at my hotel I damn well came. We both did. More than once. Throughout the night. Suddenly I was seeing the Eden in a brand new light.

"What do you think?" Tom once asked me about some boy he was considering buying out. "Is he clean?"

"Dunno," I replied. "I have a friend who always checks their teeth. The way they do with horses. Strikes me as gross, but I suppose there's something to it."

The Sea Hag was my bag. For Tom one visit

was enough. TVs were welcome, and the overall atmosphere was decidedly effeminate. That's where I met little Dang. Originally from the north of the country, he knew from an early age that at heart he was more girl than boy. As with many such Thai youths, his parents readily accepted the obvious and allowed him to cross-dress. And thus another *katoy* was born. Small and lithe, he'd initially moved to Bangkok hoping to become a classical dancer. But needing to make money, he soon turned to prostitution. Half of what he earned he sent to his family.

Little Dang and tall Dang were friends. With each aware that the other was also my lover. I never encountered any jealousy on the Bangkok gay scene, and certainly not among Thais. Knowing how voracious my sexual appetite could be, whenever little Dang went to visit his family, he would introduce me to a boy I could always count on for sex.

"He'll be at the Sea Hag every night until I come back, just in case."

The only such boy I ever found need of walked off with my expensive watch in the morning. When I told Dang, he was more upset than I was. I figured the kid felt I could afford it. He was right. That same afternoon I bought a new one. And in 1973 hocked it in Munich. I've not worn a wristwatch since.

Dang never returned from one of those sojourns in the north.

"Dang's dead!" tall Dang cried out the moment I opened the door he'd been pounding on.

Dead was putting it mildly. He'd been decapitated.

In yet another dreadful bus accident. The usual scenario. Madcap driver recklessly screeching round precarious curves, oblivious to oncoming traffic or equally reckless vehicles trying to pass. Then instantly fleeing, leaving the bus and however many dead or injured passengers behind. And when found by the cops and arrested? The bus company pays a bribe, the driver is set free, and that's that. Compensation for the victims or their kinfolk? Forget it.

Dang and I attended the Buddhist services, but not the cremation. According to the monks, that was exclusively for family members. Little Dang was gone. Life goes on. Tall Dang and I went home and made love. (As it happens, Tennessee also lost a male lover to decapitation. His name was Bill. Only in that tragic instance the culprit was a subway train.)

Best for dancing was the Fandango. Sometimes Tom went with me. I'd dance while he scouted and chatted up. Even now I can hear "Let It Be" and "Bridge Over Troubled Waters" playing. Feel my steps slowing and me holding my dancing partner oh-so-tightly.

"I'm going to Pattaya with Oliver for a few days," Tennessee informed me over dinner one evening. "I'm told it's very gay. I'll write and let you know!"

Oliver being Tom's traveling companion, Oliver Evans. The professor. Whom I never got to meet. Well, did and didn't. He was at the press conference, namelessly. We weren't introduced. In the play I call him A Close Friend. I haven't a clue where he was staying. Definitely not the Oriental. A shadowy figure. One reads-tell about him, but without gleaning much solid info. In 1950 he published a poems book, *Young Man with a Screwdriver*, foreword by Tennessee Williams. He's mentioned twice in the *Memoirs*. The first time, harking back to events of the late 1940s, Tom refers to him as "my dear friend Professor Oliver Evans." And he appears near the end, when Tom is still writing away and again switches to the present (something he does regularly right through the *Memoirs*), which at that point is ca. 1973 in San Juan, Puerto Rico. His pen is reliving the deep depression he fell prey to following the death of his years-long lover Frank Merlo. But now he is depressed by the situation of "my oldest and closest friend, Professor Oliver Evans," who is gravely ill. Evans survived that, and only died in 1981, aged 66. His other published works include a biography of Carson McCullers and a New Orleans guidebook. He was present when Tom had dinner with Mishima in Yokohama, and later wrote about it for the May 1972 issue of *Esquire* magazine, an article titled "A Pleasant Evening with Yukio Mishima." Some of Tom's letters to Oliver are in *The Selected Letters of Tennessee Williams*, as well as in various university archives. And that's about it.

What I do know is that Tom was footing the bill for both of them. Know because Tom wrote and told me. Yes, those letters are gone. But certain typewritten lines remain indelibly imprinted in my memory.

"It is indeed very gay here. Not that it's doing me

any good. Oliver is keeping all the boys to himself! What gratitude. I take him on a luxurious ocean cruise, pay for everything, and now he won't let me get laid. I can't wait to get back to Bangkok and go out on the town with you."

He'd close by typing his name: "Love, Tom"; though not signing it. We'd become friends, but I was still a newspaperman. Nor did he later elaborate on Oliver. The one time I brought up his name, Tom shrugged and changed the subject.

Ah, but while Tom was pining for sex in Pattaya, I *was* getting laid. And not by going to the bars, or one of the Dangs coming round or anything. A young Malay lad had just started as a copyboy at the paper. He was rather pretty and I took a fancy to him. We went for lunch, got to talking, and he invited me for dinner. He was living with an aunt in a pleasant house on a quiet side street. I could tell his aunt was wary of me, but things progressed rapidly nonetheless. The next night he was in my room, sitting beside me on the bed. When I began stroking him, he smiled shyly and said: "My aunt warned me to bring some vaseline along."

"No need," I replied, "I have KY jelly."

And so we made love. Till then he'd been a virgin. A virgin who couldn't get enough of me. He wanted to do it all. Me to him, him to me. To hell with sleep, I happily obliged. But even before we stripped off our clothes, I held him by the shoulders and tried to make one thing clear, since I knew where this was heading.

"Whatever you do," I said, "do not fall in love with me."

He didn't answer. His raging hormones wouldn't allow him to hear what I was saying. By morning he was hopelessly in love. Only I wasn't. No matter how good the sex, I needed to take distance. Tom's return provided the excuse. By-and-by I found other excuses. After maybe two more times, we never had sex again. He was a sweet boy.

VI

"I'm feeling restless," Tom said over the phone when his call got put through to my desk. "I want to go to Singapore. Can you come with me? I wish you would. You know the place, right? Said you have a boyfriend there?"

"I said a lover. If I'm able to go, you'll meet her."

"You mean it's a woman? You have a girlfriend in Singapore?"

"First things first. Let me find out about going. If the paper won't pay, and give me time off for it, I don't see how it can happen. I'll get on the case right away. Tell you the verdict tonight. Dinner at the Normandie?"

"Yes, that's good. Do your best. I can chip in some. I want you with me. And I want to leave soon."

"Okay. I gotta go now. Deadlines don't take prisoners. Bye."

It wasn't an easy sell. Geoff liked the idea, and

58

said yes he could spare me for a week or so. But it wasn't up to him. Given that money was involved, it would have to be cleared by both Nick and the executive editor, Mr. Theh. And neither were interested in another Tennessee Williams piece.

"So I'll write more about Singapore. A follow-up to the supplement. There's plenty of stuff I didn't get to. Should we ask Mr. Ali?"

"Don't bother," Nick said wryly, "he'd probably say yes. I'll get Theh to sign off on it. Bring us a couple of decent features. And no Williams, y'hear? Your little play covered him just fine."

We went down by train. Tom insisted on first class. My budget wouldn't handle that, so he kicked in the difference. We had miniscule adjoining compartments. In which the first night we froze our asses off. There was no way to kill the fucking air conditioning!

"I'm an icicle," Tom said in the morning, holding himself and still shivering.

"Me, too," said I. "Brrrr. Ain't it great what money can buy?"

The second-class carriage we switched to for the rest of the journey was sufficiently comfortable. Even with black soot from the coal-fired steam engine occasionally flying in through the open windows. For much of the day Tom sat in a seat across the aisle from mine, typing on his portable. I took photos. One was a nifty profile shot of him smiling at the sheet of paper in the typer while writing. More eventual fuel for my Bali renunciation pyre. Ditto the candid snap of Tom in the hotel pool, wearing a rubber bathing cap. There were two-tier bunk beds above our seats. We arrived in Singapore reasonably refreshed and hopped in a taxi.

"Raffles Hotel," Tom told the driver.

"The Raffles?" I said.

"Yes, I know. Your budget. Don't fret, I'll help with that."

We asked for two rooms on the same floor. Tom wrote 'Thomas Williams' on the registration form, and gave his occupation as 'writer.' Did the desk clerk recognize him? Whether or not, he decided to charge Tom a third more than me.

"What's this?" said Tom. "Is my room bigger than his?"

"Well, no..."

"Well nothing. I want the same rate he's paying."

"Yes, sir. My apologies. I made a mistake."

"You certainly did," Tom retorted, his lips slightly curled in annoyance. "Now have someone show us to our rooms."

"Yes, sir," the young clerk meekly replied. And then loudly called out: "Bellhop!"

"Let's dump our luggage and unpack later," Tom said as we were led down the hallway. "I need a breath of freshness. This place is beginning to feel stuffy."

Once out front we hailed a bicycle trishaw.

"Where to?" asked the driver.

"Anywhere," said Tom. "Just start pedaling, we're in your hands. Then take us back to the hotel."

Trishaws cost a pittance. Even those that hover in wait by the Raffles. After paying the driver what he asked, Tom dug into his pocket and gave the man every penny of loose change he had.

"Let the Raffles put that in their pipe and smoke it," he growled.

Tennessee Williams may have been a millionaire, but he wasn't a fool. And he disliked being treated as one. As for his generosity of spirit, that famous line about 'the kindness of strangers' didn't spring out of thin air.

"Come to my room quick," Tom shrieked while half running into mine. "We're checking out of here pronto!"

Scampering around near the foot of his bed were three sizeable cockroaches. I could empathize with Tom being freaked out. I had my own history with these irksome critters. One that didn't get resolved until Bombay, 1974...long after I'd recoiled, frightened, when a Hong Kong whore dared me to reach under her skirt and retrieve a roach she'd plucked off the floor and teasingly placed against her crotch. Yet by this time, watching Tom back away in horror from the trio of insects, I was slowly coming to terms with them.

"They're really quite harmless," I said.

"They're disgusting. Go pack. I've had my fill of the illustrious Raffles. Oh, and I hope you'll write about them."

"Only if I want to make people laugh. The cockroach isn't exactly an alien in this neck of the woods. It's a mammoth task for the most hygienic establishments to keep them at bay. Even the Air Force couldn't banish them from their super-clean kitchens when I was in Texas doing my basic training."

"All well and good. But we're leaving!"

We left. Took a taxi to some other hotel recommended in Tom's guidebook. Thankfully the rooms were roach-free. Yet that night there was a dead one smack-dab on top of Tom's steak. He sent it back and made do with the salad. We didn't check out.

A cockroach also thwarted Tom's one attempt to again ask about my Singapore lover. By flying headlong into his face.

"Tell me about your..." Thwack!

"Get used to them, Tom," I said. "And learn how to duck. C'mon, let's move to a table where there's more light. Maybe they'll leave us alone. Although with these Asian buggers it's hard to tell."

We were on Bugis Street. Smoking marijuana, drinking beer, ducking cockroaches. And viewing a nonstop parade of drop-dead gorgeous drag queens. I'm not sure who was more astonished: Tom, finding it hard to believe what his ever-widening eyes were seeing; or me witnessing his bewilderment. One of the three greatest American playwrights of the 20th century; a man who in his writings had explored every crevice of human emotions; who had plumbed the depths of the human heart and soul; who was no stranger to the weird bends and twists of sexuality. Deposit this same Tennessee Williams in an obscure hideaway of delightful decadence and a few transvestite whores are throwing him for a loop? Tom was too absorbed to notice me shaking my head.

"I don't know what to make of this," I could hear him saying under his breath.

"Maybe make it the subject of your next play," I replied in an equally muted tone.

I'd turned away from him by then. My ears were listening, but my eyes were glued to the sisters' enchanting beauty.

"My next play..."

There was more astonishment in store. Oodles of it.

"We're going on a date, Tom," I told him a couple of days later.

"We are? Says who?"

"Says me. Tonight. With my lover and a friend of hers. Cool, eh? You'll finally get to meet Kim. She'll ring me shortly and tell me where to meet them and what time."

I'd gone to Katong the morning before to sound out Kim and Amanda on what I had in mind. And if they agreed (which they did in an instant), make the necessary arrangements and let me know. A nice restaurant, I told them. Not too flashy, or over-the-top expensive, but with very good red wine. I even printed Château Margaux on a slip of paper and said they should ask. And failing that, something comparable.

"Kim," said Tom. "Her name is Kim. And she is..."

"A drag queen, Thomas. A stunningly beautiful ladyboy. As is her friend Amanda. Don't go backing out on me now, it's all set up. Trust me on this, okay? You'll love them. And as usual we'll split the bill," I added with a wink.

"Hmm, okay. What's to lose..."

"Not your virginity, that's for sure," I said with a laugh. "Besides, they do have cocks and assholes!"

The girls were already seated at a corner table when Tom and I arrived. And this time Tom's eyes widened with admiration. It was immediately apparent that he was taken by these ladies, and particularly Kim.

"You were right," he whispered in my ear, "she really is beautiful."

I introduced them. They all shook hands.

"So pleased to make your acquaintance," Tom said to both at once.

We started with vodka martinis, and while sipping and chatting made our selections and ordered separately. Tom of course chose the wine. Château Margaux wasn't listed, but he did find a satisfactory substitute.

"And what do you, ah, ladies do, if I may ask?" Tom inquired.

"We're whores," Amanda replied bluntly and without batting an eye.

Amanda was a tall, dark-skinned Malay, pleasingly muscular of arm, with long black hair, and rivetingly sloe-eyed.

"I see," said Tom, dabbing his lips with a napkin.

"I know you do," was Amanda's gentle response. Her voice was low and husky, her eyes were smiling, and now her right hand was resting on Tom's forearm. She leaned forward, gradually forcing the uppermost curve of her ample breasts to tease themselves toward Tom from the top of the low-cut dress she was wearing. Tom was clearly intrigued. And me even more so. 'Will he give it a go?' I could hear myself wondering. Kim squeezed my hand under the table, telling me she was thinking the same thing.

"Yes," said Tom, recovering his composure. "And you're making out all right with that? I mean financially."

"We survive," Amanda assured him. "Ask Eddie. He lived with us for... What was it, Eddie? Three months?"

I nodded affirmatively. And kissing Kim flush on the lips said, "I'll never stop missing it."

That got us off the whores hook. We spoke some about my time in Katong, with Tom occasionally asking a question or interjecting a droll comment. Then he and Amanda got to conversing, just the two of them, while Kim and I discussed what the four of us might do together in the coming days. Except that four soon became three. Which funnily enough caught me off guard. They seemed to be getting on so well. Amanda was asking about his writing (Tom had no problem with them knowing who he was). And at one point I overheard her saying she'd read him and knew the films, but had never been to the theater.

"Have they even done me here?" he asked himself more than her. "I'll have to find out."

We'd finished dinner and were drinking cognacs and nibbling on chocolates. Kim and Amanda excused themselves and went to the ladies room.

"I can't, baby," Tom said to me soberly. "She's sweet, but I can't. What do you do with them anyway?"

"I don't know what you do, Tom," I replied. "I've never watched you. Or you me. I know what I do, though. Damn near everything!"

"It's been a lovely evening," Tom said when the girls returned. "Thank you. But I'm a bit tired. Martinis, wine, brandy. The bill is paid. We'll take you home in a taxi."

"Katong," Kim told the driver.

"Whoopee, no cockroach!" I exclaimed.

"No what?" said a startled Tom.

"Private joke, Thomas," I said, giving Kim a peck on the cheek.

When we got to Katong, only Amanda alighted from the cab.

"Kim is coming to the hotel with me," I informed Tom.

Hotel.

Lift.

Room.

Undress.

Bed.

"Fuck me, Eddie. Fuck me. Fuck meeeeeeeeee........!"

*

66

I saw no need to query Tom on his unwillingness to bed Amanda. I'd made a stab at nudging him past his customary predilections and it didn't pan out. His sexual limits and quirks were his business, not mine. If he felt any aversion, it wasn't to her personally. And certainly not to Kim, as would be borne out over the ensuing days. Yet had I realized at the time that Tom's feelings were riddled with political concerns, I would have been happy to discuss that with him. Or even debate. But it took reading the *Memoirs* to open those doors.

In short, Tennessee Williams had outgrown an overtly camp youth and was now thoroughly converted to what he understood gay liberation to be all about. A conversion he credited to the "discreetly organized gay world of New York," and then in New Orleans went "proselytizing my 'gay' friends in the Quarter to conduct themselves in a fashion that was not just a travesty of the other sex." For him, Gay Lib was a "serious crusade" in which camp mannerisms had no place. He viewed extreme forms of swish and camp as "products of self-mockery" that could only serve to give homosexuals a bad name. And even prevent its practitioners from getting their own rocks off. "That type of behavior," he writes, "made them distasteful, sexually, to anyone interested in sex." Adding that it was "obnoxious" and destined to disappear. Goodness gracious, how I wish dear Tom had said that to me and Kim. Or better still, recited it to our passionately entwined bodies...while watching us fuck!

Tom's views in this regard were more than misguided, they were warped. And his behavioral prescription for the health and well-being of queerdom cockamamie. What he construed as self-mockery is on the contrary a true expression of how some people are and want to be. And in certain significant contexts can be as politically valid as the best aspects of feminism, both gay and straight. Yet there was and is an ideological battle raging. One that I saw played out ferociously live in late-1970s London, at the ICA (Institute of Contemporary Arts).

Tennessee would have loved Gay Sweatshop, and rightly so. A serious theater company with definite aims and boasting a wealth of talented male & female writers, directors and actors. Whose productions over more than two decades made a lasting mark. Blue Lips, aka The Brixton Fairies, were also serious. But to some sensibilities they came across as frivolous. Which they knew, and as 'flaming queens with a purpose' meant to. They openly flaunted what Tennessee was preaching against. In their day-to-day lives because that's who they were. And in their theater performances as entertainment and to make a statement. 'Swish-camp is okay,' is what they were saying. And saying it in a way that unmistakably poked fun at the very notion of outré-faggy lifestyles being derided as unacceptable self-mockery. Lighthearted satire though it was, it oftentimes got up some people's noses. Gay Sweatshop were by no means overly-solemn zealots, but Blue Lips did irk them.

I don't know who started it, or if there was an actual trigger. It could have been spontaneous combustion. Their ideological differences provided kindling enow for that. The two troupes were performing on the same evening. Both had appreciative audiences. But once the seriousness and the fun were over and done with, all hell broke loose. Backstage the rival groups unceremoniously set about smashing up each other's props. Another way of making a statement. 'Take that, you silly-ass poofs.' 'Up yours, you fascist queers.' And so on. Pity they didn't team up later and turn it into a play. Rave reviews, darlings!

Am I biased? You bet I am! A close friend of mine (to this day) was in Gay Sweatshop, and I'd attended a number of their productions. *As Time Goes By* was especially memorable. But it was The Brixton Fairies' communal squat on Railton Road, a stone's throw from where I lived with my girlfriend, that I took to visiting. Their radical gay approach to dealing with homosexual issues was right up my philosophical alley. But most of all I simply adored their queen of queens, Julian Hows, who was as politically astute as he was physically luscious. Madly in love with the boy, was I. And uncontrollably lusting after him whenever we met. All that stood in the way of consummation was my unaccountable shyness in letting my feelings be known.

Now dear reader, please do allow me a delectably precious Julian anecdote before we dash back to Singapore and rejoin Tennessee and Kim. Julian was employed as a platform conductor on the London Underground, the Tube. And when London Transport (LT) introduced a new uniform policy, permitting female staff to wear trousers if they wished, Julian decided it should work both ways. And so one day arrived at Earls Court station clad in a grey two-piece LT skirt and top. Management were outraged.

*

"I hope your friend wasn't offended," Tom said to Kim when she came to collect us two days after the night before. "I really was beat."

"Not about that," Kim replied. "I'd already sensed we weren't your type. I told Amanda that when we were in the loo. What did niggle was her hearing you say something to Eddie about an odor? You could have kept your voice down. And anyway, Amanda is a scrupulously clean person."

"Sorry. Maybe it was her cologne, or the soap she uses. I'm sensitive to smells. My nostrils tickled," he said touching his nose. "But you're right, I ought to have been more careful. So where are we going then? And by the way, you are very pretty, even when you're...not dressed up."

"Thank you," said Kim. "I like you, too. And Amanda liked you."

We spent three days going all around Singapore. Kim showing Tom the sights in a way I couldn't have, even though I was familiar with many of the areas we explored. Only not Sago Lane and the death houses, that was new to me. Most had been demolished by the end of the 1960s, but a few still stood. Places where the destitute dying who had no one to care for them went or were taken to pass their final days. The barest of dormitory quarters upstairs, funeral parlors on the ground floor. These flanked by shops selling death paraphernalia (fake money, paper model cars and houses, etc; all to be burned, so the deceased could take them along into the afterlife). Parallel to Sago Lane is Sago Street, which in the past was renowned for its brothels.

Kim and I waited hidden from the noonday sun under a shop awning while Tom went charging up and down rickety stairs, investigating.

"A writer wants to see everything!" he said when he was done.

"Good," I replied. "And now that you have, you can tell us about it over lunch. Let's go find somewhere. Don't ask me why, but this death business has given me an appetite. I'm famished."

It was pure joy seeing Tom and Kim getting along so famously. Wherever we went, they'd be chatting away. And laughing. Tom had an infectious laugh. And a broad smile that was invariably made brighter by the way his eyes sparkled. They were like two school kids on a class outing. I even saw them holding hands. So yeah, he liked Kim a lot, her ultra-camp mannerisms notwithstanding. Still... And for this I need to jump ahead in time. With Tom and me back in Bangkok. Standing outside the different hotel (i.e., not the Oriental) he'd decided to check into. When out of the blue he looks up at me and says: "Baby, if you like them that swish, you like girls."

"Oh, but I do, Tom" said I. "I surely do."

Kim spent most of my remaining Singapore nights at the hotel with me. There were no gay bars that we knew of, or safe cruising spots we could direct Tom to. And Bugis Street was a one-off for him, as with the Sea Hag in Bangkok. So we three would dine at the hotel or a nearby restaurant, chat for a spell over drinks, then go to our rooms. As you can imagine, Kim and I made the most of our time in mine!

"What's the matter, Tom?"

Kim had left, I'd gone to join him for lunch, and found him with his head in his hands, blankly nursing a martini. I sat down, but he stayed hunched over his drink.

"I don't know what to do with my life," he said without looking up.

Now, you hear that from the mouth of a friend and you feel compassion, your heart sympathizes. And that did come, was even already there. But something else leapt to the fore first. Profound relief. As though a tremendous weight had lifted itself off my head. For I too had been wrestling with bouts of uncertainty over what direction I wanted my life to take. Yet now there's a voice inside me saying: 'If Tennessee Williams [who by then had won two Pulitzer Prizes and four New York Drama Circle Critics' awards] doesn't know what to do with his

72

life, why should I worry?!'

And no, I didn't tell this to Tom. I just let that thought, and the sense of liberation that accompanied it, sink into my being and do its work. All the while knowing that as much as I empathized with Tom, I was also blessing him. Thanks to him and his plight, and having the courage to so candidly express it, he had verily set me free. Of myself.

No wonder Tom was at loose ends. He'd been through a long bad patch, from which he was still tentatively emerging. Frank Merlo's death from lung cancer in 1963 had left him devastated. Always fond of drinking, his reliance on alcohol increased at an alarming rate. As did his consumption of amphetamines and the barbiturate Seconal. For the rest of the decade he seesawed between nightmarish depression and near-amnesia. He kept writing, but in retrospect marveled that he was able to and barely remembered what. On at least one occasion when a television journalist and camera crew came to interview him, he fell flat on his face immediately upon opening the door. All this and more Tom spoke about with ease during our numerous conversations. Sometimes peppered with flashes of humor. He wasn't bitter. He accepted the past and felt he was learning from it. Which didn't necessarily make the uncertainties of the unfolding future any less troubling. Especially for an artist, a real artist, it's not what you've done that counts, or how professionally successful you've been. It's what you are doing now and will do that matters.

I ordered a Campari soda, allowed him to indulge in his glum mood for a while longer, and then said: "I don't believe you."

Now he was looking at me!

"What don't you believe?" he asked sharply.

The waiter brought my drink, I proposed a toast 'to life,' and we clinked glasses.

"Don't believe what?" he asked again.

"What you said," I replied calmly. "You damn well do know. You're doing it. You're writing."

"Smartass!" he shot back. And called out to the waiter to bring another martini.

Writing, yes. But with his plays (for Williams was also a novelist, short-story writer, and an accomplished poet) moving in other directions than what theater critics and the public were wanting from him. More poetic and experimental directions. He had in no way lost his artistic grip. That remained as strong as when he was penning the highly acclaimed works that had brought him fame and fortune. Only it would take until after his own death in 1983 for this to be widely recognized. Indeed, Tennessee Williams had always been poetic and experimental! As well as deeply concerned with the human condition.

He once advised me to write plays, saying: "That's where the money is." Yet that isn't why he was writing. He'd made his money, and continuing royalties ensured he would keep on making it. No matter if the critics were out to get him (and they were!) or new plays folded within weeks of opening. He tried his best to shrug off unfavorable notices, and in his heart knew he should. But when you're in the public eye and the hawks are circling, that's often easier thought and said than done.

In the *Memoirs* Tom says: "I am lucky at real estate, lucky at cards: also sometimes at love." And then goes on to call himself a "wasted dude." Adding that his "adventures in theater have failed more often than not." Which wasn't really so. Although now in his sixties, and with seven years all but lost, it was beginning to feel like that.

His passing bouts of gloom aside, Tom was also thankful that the suspected breast cancer which had prompted Harry's press conference question about 'coming to Bangkok to die' was instead gynecomastia (enlargement of the male mammary gland) and could be easily operated on. The procedure, performed by a Thai army surgeon, took about an hour. When it was over, Tom knocked back a swig of sherry and went off with a small entourage of Thai youths to feast on steak *au poivre* and vintage wines.

*

Having done the train going down, Tom decided we should fly back to Bangkok. My budget consented to an economy-class ticket, whereas Tom opted for first class. Midway through the flight he came to see how I was, but also to tell me about the fabulous meal they'd been served in his sequestered section of the aircraft. He was all smiles and happily patting his tummy whilst describing it to me. Until I pricked his balloon by truthfully telling him that we 'peons' had eaten precisely the same thing.

"Oh," he said. "Our seats are more comfortable, though." With which he ambled off to go sit in his for the duration.

Declaring that he'd had his fill of "that stinking river" (the Chao Phraya, alongside which the Oriental Hotel is situated), Tom ordered the baggage he'd left behind brought to the more modest hotel he now checked into. Thereby sacrificing a view of boats and barges and the skyline of Thonburi for the sake of his sensitive nostrils. His room was small compared to the suite he'd given up, but adequate for the remainder of his stay. He had tossed his Singapore luggage on the bed and was methodically unpacking it.

"Ah, look what I have!" he said gleefully, waving a fully stuffed zip-lock bag at me.

"I hope that's not what I think it is," was my unbelieving response.

"Yes," he replied. "It's the rest of the stash you and Kim gave me. I only smoked a thin joint or two every other day. And their grass is so good. Clever of me, no?"

I was gobsmacked.

"You're fuckin' nuts!" I said. "Forget that it's like bringing coals to Newcastle, which it is. Do you have any idea what woulda' happened if they'd searched your bags at customs?"

"But I thought..."

"Thought what? That dope is legal here? Or in

76

Singapore? Or anywhere in Southeast Asia. What a firsthand scoop I'd have had: 'Tennessee Williams busted in Bangkok for smuggling marijuana.' Not to mention the bundle of bread it would have cost you in bribes. Jesus Mary."

"So what should we do now?" Tom asked confusedly.

"Smoke a joint, what else. Here, gimme that," I said, snatching the baggy from his hand. "You get on with your unpacking, I'll roll."

I didn't see much of Tom between then and when he left. I'd come down with paratyphoid and was sick in bed. A bummer with an upside to it, since it got me out of the Singapore stories I didn't feel like writing anyway. Once I was on my feet and back at my desk there were other assignments waiting. Singapore had been forgotten. No one even asked how my trip was! Tom would phone to check on me, and one time came by the hotel. He'd had to change his plans and sail to the States rather than Europe, where he was intending to go. That voyage was too long, all around Africa via the Cape of Good Hope.

"I don't understand why we can't go through the Suez Canal," he said.

"Because it's blocked," I answered.

"Since when? How come?"

"Since 1967. The Six-Day War, remember? Israel, the Arabs. No, you don't. You were deep in your fog then."

"Yes."

So instead he sailed to San Francisco aboard the

Tennessee Williams

S.S. President Wilson. We said our goodbyes in his room. He gave me a colorful paisley necktie.

"Your queens will love you with this on," he said, winking.

I gave him a light kiss on the lips.

"Well, that was overdue, wouldn't you say?"

"I didn't want to get your hopes up," I replied smilingly.

A porter came for his bags. We all went down in the lift. Tom's taxi was waiting. He got in and rolled down the window. We waved to one another as the cab pulled away and then sped off. Bon voyage, Tennessee Williams. Tom.

*

A friend dropped by the other day, and in the course of conversation inquired how my book was coming along. This book. I said fine, but I still had plenty of writing to do. Whereupon he asked a question that had never been put to me before.

"Were you ever intimate with Tennessee?"

The discerning reader will already know my answer. If Tom and I had been intimate, I'd have said by now.

"I'm sure it never crossed either of our minds," I further replied. "We weren't each other's type."

"Type, not type," my friend said. "What about Gore Vidal and Jack Kerouac?"

"That I can see. Clearly. But you're right. When it comes to sex, anything is possible. And should be. Only I was into young feminine boys. And even when on my 'best behavior,' I was too feminine for Tennessee. We simply weren't drawn to one another in that way. Sometimes it's better like that. You don't have to fuck everyone."

My sexual tastes in women are incredibly eclectic. And over the years have grown more so. Also regarding what I'm up for doing with them in bed. As long as it's consensual, the sky is the limit. Not so with males. Macho frightens me. My asshole closes tight, my mouth clamps shut, and my cock retreats. 'Don't you dare touch me,' my body screams out. It happened in Bangkok, at one of John Fowler's insanely wild parties. John, the queen of men's fashion. Who had done so much to promote upcountry tribal fabrics. And whose shop was a prime sponsor of my radio program. But who was otherwise totally fucking mad! Thick candles, enormously high, burned brightly all over the grounds and on both sides of the klong (canal) that ran through his property. Huge fireworks kept streaming loudly into the sultry night air. With John drunkenly parading about, followed closely by a similarly half-clad bevy of young Thai males. It was a big gathering... Westerners, Thais, a few Chinese, none of them older than early middle-age. I don't recall any women.

I watched for a while from a safe distance, sipping a cool drink. Then wandered into the empty house and set about admiring the tapestries hanging everywhere in its several large rooms. When without even the warning of approaching footsteps I got grabbed from behind and pushed against the wall.

"I want you, and I want you now," said a voice that was too rough for my liking. As was the burly physique that was pressing itself on me after I'd been jerked around to face my assailant. He leaned in and tried to kiss me. I struggled to get away, but his superior strength maintained a tight grasp.

"Oh, I see. You'd rather be taken, is it? That's what all you pansies like. Okay, we'll do it that way. It'll make fucking you more fun."

With which he began trying to undress me. Even while alternately groping for my cock and taking his out. He was sweating and his breath was putrid with the rancid odor of warm beer gone stale in his gut. Then lateral inspiration took over. I stopped squirming and reached a hand into his open fly and found his balls. Feigning erotic delirium, I held them tenderly. And in a gentle sighing tone said, "Do you really want me? All of me?"

"Hell, yeah," he replied. "I want to fuck you silly."

"Good," I said. And in the same moment squeezed his nuts as hard as I could. He yelled out, backed off, and doubled over. And I wasted no time in running as fast as I could.

Years later, in San Francisco, I wasn't so lucky. I did get raped. By a guy in drag, no less. With whom I'd gone willingly, back to his place. After we'd picked each other up in a late-night luncheonette. I was expecting sex, yes. That was the whole point. But not to get unceremoniously thrown face down onto a mattress in an oversized closet, my trousers yanked off, my hands held fast behind my back by one of his, and while he's banging away at my bum holding another hand over my mouth to prevent me from screaming. He was a tall, strong dude. Very black. With three black friends playing cards in the main room and listening in (the walls were cardboard thin). On top of which, whilst screwing the shit out of me...I mean full throttle deep penetration with a very long and bolt-hard member...he also managed to pick my wallet clean.

"Did you like that, honey?" he asked sweetly after he'd shot his load.

I was too stunned to reply. Just stood and pulled up my jeans. He took me in his arms and said, "Come meet my friends."

They nodded hello and continued with their card game.

"Maybe you want to go now?" he said. "It's getting late."

Still dazed, I mumbled my reply.

"Yes, go. Sounds like a plan."

"Oh dear," he said when we got down to the street, "I'll have to give you money for a taxi. You don't have any, not even for a bus. And by now they've stopped running. Look, there's a cab. Just tell the driver what address and I'll pay the fare. And listen," he continued while hugging me, "I'd really like to see you again. Look for me in that coffee shop when you're next in the neighborhood. Yes?"

"Yes. Sure. Bye." Huh?

Four years earlier, in 1976, I had a series of close

calls hitchhiking through the Southwest. Car stops, I hop in, and within minutes the redneck creep driving starts making a play.

"Boy, I woke up with such a hard-on this morning," went one opening line. "You must get awfully lonely sometimes," was another. Followed by a grope. Soon as I say no, we screech to a halt and I'm standing in the middle of nowhere gazing at cacti and tumbleweeds but with no cars in sight. The only time I did say yes was when I got to Louisiana and a good-looking black fellow politely asked if he could suck me off.

"Fine," I said, "Pull over and we'll do it."

He did, I dug it, and five rides later I was in New Orleans. Nothing untoward occurred when after two weeks I split the Big Easy and thumbed my way along the eastern seaboard to Philadelphia, and from there caught a train to New York. I did, however, spend a most pleasant night with a voluptuous coed in Tuscaloosa, Alabama.

Rape sucks. My sexual fantasies are way out there, but taking someone by force against their will has never been among them. Nor could my cock manage it. Even with consensual sex, the slightest hint of real resistance and it goes limp. If a chick wants it that rough, she'll have to tell me first. And no, I won't do rough sex with guys. Or S&M. In my repertoire of kinky tricks, both are for indulging in with ladies only.

Every one of us is innately bisexual. All animals are. Whether we know it or not. Or rather, choose to acknowledge the fact. And that's what's important, the acknowledging. Accepting that regardless of how our brain's like/dislike mechanism has till now been functioning, somewhere along the line we could feel ourselves sexually attracted to someone of the same gender. Acting on it is another matter. And too complicated to discuss here. Just never say never, is all. Not if you want to stay mentally healthy. Or to accurately paraphrase a certain wise teacher of tantra, 'Your attitude towards sex reveals everything about your whole life.'

Tennessee knew he was bisexual. He'd had that one affair with a woman, a carnal adventure he so thoroughly enjoyed that decades later he relished writing about it: "I took to it like a duck to water. She changed positions with me, she got on top...and rode my cock like a hobbyhorse and then she came and I'd never imagined such a thing, all that hot wet stuff exploding inside her and about my member and her gasping hushed outcries." After that he tried dating other females. While already in puberty he felt his sexual desire aroused by a girl who remained a close companion for 11 years. But once his emotional transmission shifted gears, he also knew that he now preferred making it with men. All this without ever denying either aspect of his sexuality.

I am knowingly queer and I am knowingly straight. I am a human sexual. And I love the word 'queer'!

Sex and sexuality. I must admit that there's a ring of truth to what the courtesan Chrysis says to her philosopher friend Naucrates in *Aphrodite*, Pierre Louÿs' sublime novel about life and love in ancient Alexandria.

Chrysis: "When it comes to love, woman is the perfect instrument. From head to foot she is made simply and marvelously for love. She alone knows how to love. She alone knows how to be loved. Consequently, if a loving couple consists of two women it is perfect. If it has only one, it is half as good. And if it has none, it is utterly ridiculous. That's all."

Naucrates: "You are hard on Plato, my girl."

Chrysis: "Like the gods, great men are not great in every respect...Sophocles couldn't paint. Plato didn't know how to love. And those philosophers, poets and rhetoricians who follow Plato are no better than he was. They may be admirable in their own arts, but in love they are ignoramuses."

Rings true why? And to me of all people! Tennessee already answered that for you, when he said I like girls. And me, when I called myself a lesbian. Nor is there anything more heavenly to my eyes than the sight of two women making love. The female body is indeed perfect.

There's another of my drag-queen lovers whom I dearly wish Tom could have met. Not only met, but seen in the nude. And been with us the time we went down for breakfast in the Viengtai. Her name was Sue Ling. And she was ravishingly beautiful. Moreover, simply by looking at her you would never know Sue was a boy. Stark naked and facing you, whether standing or lying down, and with her cock tucked firmly between her thighs, she appeared every inch a girl. Her face, her abundantly full bosom, everything about her. Even I would occasionally find myself doing a double-take when she'd suddenly get an erection.

So Sue and I stroll into the dining room, where I catch sight of Carl sitting with a male friend I'd not seen before. Carl waves that we should join them, which we do. Sue was wearing jeans shorts and a thin blouse with the top three buttons undone and nothing underneath. And the whole time we're there, whatever desultory we got to talking about, this guy couldn't take his eyes off Sue. They were like glued. With all the rest of him exuding unmitigated lust. And the more he ogled, the more Carl kept smiling. And now and then winking at me. And the next day told me why. His friend was an out-and-out homophobe. Who never tired of saying how much he hated queers.

"Boy, she's hot," he'd said to Carl as soon as Sue and I were gone.

"Want to fuck her, do you?" Carl replied.

"Hell yes! For a dip into that I'd even pay."

"Really? But I thought screwing boys wasn't your thing."

"Say what! You don't mean...?"

"Yeah, you dumb fuck. All cock and balls male. But with tits for good measure. Should I ask Eddie if he can fix you up with her?"

I am absolutely certain that Tom would have gotten a real kick out of that. Seeing yet another hypocrite choke on their own stupidity. As would Gore Vidal have.

"He's always doing that, using my name," Tennessee riposted in Singapore, of an afternoon when we were browsing the book racks in a newsagent's and I held up a paperback edition of Vidal's *Sex, Death, and Money*, saying: "Oh look, Gore mentions you in the introduction to this." Which is pretty much what Gore later said about Tom using his name! No hypocrisy there, only a certain kind of catty affection. And mutual respect.

VII

I don't know that I thought much about Tom after he left. Although it appears we did write some while I was still in Thailand. There's mention of it in the only surviving (carbon) copy of a letter from me to him, a computer scan of which I was able to get from my archive at Stanford University. It's dated July 1st 1981, and I have good reason to believe it never reached Tom. I should have stuck to the Key West address, his house on Duncan Street. Since the alternate he'd sent me in 1971, after he'd fallen out with his longtime literary agent and friend Audrey Wood, proved useless. International Creative Management probably binned it. And you, Tom, maybe shoulda' stuck with Audrey. As a writer you made yourself, but she made your name as a playwright.

Funny, but I mention in that letter telling Brion Gysin the anecdote about Tennessee saying he didn't know what to do with his life. And Brion insisting that Tom was putting me on. Either way, the end result was the same. We both moved on with our lives. Plus I reckon Brion was wrong.

My Bangkok life got so busy. I had little time for anything apart from what I was involved with then. And practically none for correspondence. The one other person with whom I had intermittent postal contact was Kim. Even my mother hadn't heard from me in such a long time that she started harassing the State Department to find me. Resulting in a telephone call from the American Embassy.

"Mr. Woods, please write to your mother. Or maybe phone her. She's worried sick. She's also driving us crazy. Thank you."

This would happen again in the mid-1970s when I was living in Iran and working as both the sports and night editor for the *Tehran Journal*. Only then the embassy chap who rang was one of my readers, and felt terribly embarrassed by having to make the call. I quickly set his mind at ease.

"No worries, my friend. That's how it is with me and Mother. I'll send her a postcard. And hey, I'm pleased to hear you like the stuff I write."

I stayed at the *Bangkok Post* for about a year. During that time editor Nick arranged for me to replace him as *The New York Times*' Bangkok stringer (working under none other than the redoubtable Henry Kamm) while he went on a three-month holiday. I accepted an offer from ABC Radio News in New York to be their Thailand correspondent. I was freelancing for newspapers and magazines in Hong Kong, Australia, and elsewhere. I said yes when Radio Thailand asked me to read the world news six nights a week on their English-language service. And concurrently host a three-hour weekly radio show, *Sunday Potpourri* (music, poetry, interviews). And the more extracurricular work I signed up for, the more the *Post* kept asking of me. 'Eddie, we're in a jam. Write tomorrow's editorial, okay?' 'Eddie, we're doing a special anti-censorship issue. How about a poem for it?' I came up with one, too. "I Am the Press," in which I likened the press to a tree that needed constant nourishment and should never be chopped down. They ran it big on one of the few pages they'd not left blank. I was also writing my own poetry. And short stories. And keeping a journal. And going to the bars. And having sex as often as I could. And... You get the picture, right? I was busy! As was my writer friend Tennessee Williams, only now on another part of the planet.

"Eddie, let's start our own features service. We've got the experience, we have connections. Whaddya reckon?"

That was my journalist colleague John Sipper talking. Sounded good. So I left the *Post* (though without abandoning any of my other activities) and we did just that, together with the newsmen Lance Woodruff and Irwin Block. We rented office space, called the operation Dateline Asia, and set about trying to make a go of it. At first we succeeded. Then Carl reappeared in my life, I brought him on board, and the whole shebang went kerflooey. But hah, did Lance's wife ever love it whenever I came for dinner decked out in my best ultra-camp finery. I'm sure that till then he'd no idea Elizabeth was something of a fag hag!

"Eddie, what say we open a gay bar in Pattaya? The place is ripe for it, but there isn't one yet."

That was Harry Rolnick. Within a month Camelot (for the gay and gallant k/night) was up and running. Until not long afterwards it stopped running. Inevitably so. Both Harry and I were too tied up in Bangkok to spend any hands-on time in Pattaya. So we hired a manager. A really sweet black guy. Tall, handsomely slender, amiable, and queer as a three-dollar bill. And lacking in even an ounce of common sense when it came to managing anything, including his own life. A deserter from the US Army, he'd been hiding out for months as a lay devotee in a succession of Buddhist temples. I forget his name, but his ineptitude was merely strike one. Strikes two and three were on my head. Not only did I insist (over Harry's objections) that the bar be staffed entirely with pansy boys, I personally picked the cast. Which was not what the gay scene in Pattaya was hungering for. We lost a bundle on that misadventure. Harry never forgave me for it. Nor can I say I blame him. Mea culpa.

Carl in brief. Born in England during the war to an English mother and US Army master sergeant

Eddie and a technician in a Radio Thailand studio.

father. Lived with his dad in Alabama after his parents separated, returning to the UK in his later teens to study at Cambridge University. Enlisted in the British army, became a paratrooper, saw active combat duty in Cyprus, Aden, and Malaya. Got married following his discharge, had two kids, and went to work as a croupier at Charlie Chester's casino in London's Soho. There he was befriended by the author Dennis Wheatley, with whose help he fled to Germany after the infamous Kray mob threatened to put a hit on him when he refused to fork over thousands of pounds in overdue protection payments (and as a warning smashed his Jaguar to a pulp). Which is when I met him. The very first words I heard him utter were "Pizza!"

At the urging of the two Munich-based American businessmen who ran the encyclopedias scam, I took Carl on as a trainee salesman. For an entire year we drove all over Germany, never staying more than a night in any one place. Couldn't risk it. I was in full flight from my second wife, whom I loved dearly but had to leave lest one of us killed the other. And then took Carl to Asia with me, where I was planning to make a cool million selling to the Seventh Fleet. Until I said 'fuck it' and went on to do other things. Some with Carl, and some without. Our adventures were many. And despite our numerous differences, our friendship held fast. Sexually he was as straight as they come, while I (as you are well aware!) was a raging fag. Politically he was right-wing, me way to the left. I smoked dope, he wouldn't touch the stuff.

But he would roll my joints for me when we were in a hurry to go somewhere. He was also a freelance spy. For the US Air Force's OSI (Office of Special Investigations). Something I learned of only latterly, when he had no choice but to confide in me.

So now Carl was back. And in short order convinced me to expand Dateline Asia by adding an advertising department, with him running it. Which in time ruined the organization. And ultimately cost my partners every penny they'd invested. With Irwin Block alone losing 80,000 baht. Irwin, who once said that I was 'the best thing that ever happened to him.' It will take more than a mea culpa here to atone for that. At the very least it would require a personal apology. For it's not Carl I blame for Dateline Asia's downfall, but myself. Carl tried it on, I was the managing director who put his asinine idea into motion. And then allowed my own persona to change for the worse. Egomaniac worse. All me-centered. I'm in a Buddhist country, with temples everywhere in plain sight. Day after day seeing hundreds of monks on the streets with their begging bowls. And Buddha and his teachings are the farthest thing from my mind.

"Take a break from all this and go next door to the *wat* (temple)," said the young Thai lady I'd gotten to know at the government press center when I was covering a recent coup d'état for ABC News and feeling every inch a hotshot journalist.

"Why should I?"

"The Dalai Lama is visiting. It will do you good

to see him."

Her sound advice couldn't have fallen on deafer ears. The ears of someone who in his teens had immersed himself in reading books on Zen!

"You've become a real prick, Eddie. I hope you realize that."

Daryl Cantor's words. Yes, the same Daryl from those early days at the Atlanta Hotel. When we were both broke and carefree. Whom I'd now hired to sell advertising for Dateline Asia. And thus work under Carl!

"How would you feel about starting a political magazine?" Carl asked me one day. "I can arrange it for you. The financing and the distribution. International distribution. No outside editorial interference. You can write and publish whatever you like."

"But it would be left-wing," I said.

"Right. That's what we want."

"We? Oh, I get it. You mean you and your funny friends. You want to set me up to be a conduit. I can do what I like, but I'm infiltrated from the get-go. In other words a front in disguise. For drawing writers out of the woodwork so you fuckers can label them as commies. And so on. Thanks but no thanks. Which is to say, shove it!"

In the midst of all this, Eddy Rose shows up in Bangkok. One of the two Munich chaps for whom I used to sell encyclopedias. And who reckoned I owed him two grand from the time I chucked all that overboard in Hong Kong. Plus for getting me and Carl out of Manila when we were penniless and stranded there. Eddy, who once back in Germany told everyone: "Guess what. Eddie Woods turned queer!" Same as years later a gay friend was telling all and sundry in London, after learning that I was sleeping with a woman: "Good heavens. Eddie Woods turned straight!" Or as they say, you can't fucking win for losing.

"I want my money back," said Eddy.

"I don't have it," said I.

"Then I'll loan it to you," Eddy replied.

"You'll do what?"

So off to my bank we went. Where Eddy cosigned for me to borrow 2000 US dollars. Which when I got the bread (Eddy was leaving soon), I was to give to his friend Paul to give to him when Paul was next in Munich.

"Eddy mentioned that you have something for him," Paul said casually the day before his flight..

"I do. My warmest regards."

"Fine," said Paul. "It's no skin off my teeth."

Nor off mine. I was two grand richer. Since instead of repaying the bank, I let them take the money Eddy had agreed to have wired from his Swiss account as collateral. Leaving Eddy down four thou rather than the two he was seeking to recoup. And that I steadfastly insisted I didn't owe him anyway. But, Eddy and I remained friends. Only a con can truly appreciate another con. So no mea culpa there.

And then there was Jay. Eighteen years old, he'd blown into Bangkok aboard a tramp steamer from

Ceylon and somehow landed in my arms after we met in a coffee shop where he was being chatted up by half a dozen pretty girls at the same time. Chatting him up because they loved him. Loved him because he was as pretty as they were. Yet loved him more because he could fuck forever without losing his hard-on or having an orgasm. Which while he was fucking them, they'd have in multiples. Jay was incapable of ejaculating. Dug fucking okay, but mainly to please his bed partner. Who out of the kindness of his heart would every so often be female. Correct, Jay was primarily into boys. And could have earned a fortune doing both gay and hetero porn films. No pauses, no cuts; the whole nine yards in one take. Hey, maybe he did. Maybe he's still doing it.

Jay and I made it but once, and on that first night. It was '*de rigueur* that we do it,' he delighted in telling people. Though every night afterwards, until I left Bangkok three months later, he was in my bed. Usually together with two or more boys. All of us going at it like a clowder of alley cats in heat. It was a very big bed. And with Jay sharing it, and continually egging me on, my hunger for sex went through the roof. We got off on watching each other fuck or suck or doing whatever. We'd swap, we'd have threesomes, foursomes. Might as well call them galoresomes. Sex was our favorite game and we loved playing it to the hilt.

Tom would have gone for Jay. Just as I went for Floyd Anderson in San Francisco in 1976. Caught sight of him on a bus, knew in an instant that I had to have him, got off at the same stop he did, and stayed on his trail right up to his front door.

"Are you following me?" he said when he turned to face me.

"Yes."

"In that case you'd better come in," Floyd replied.

I lived with him for a couple or so weeks, before embarking on my long circuitous journey to New York, whence after a month I flew to London. Floyd was camp and masculine in equal measure. As was Jay. Come to think of it, Tom would quite easily have gone for Floyd. And when I was in bed with Jay and our playmates, I could on occasion get turned on by boys who were somewhat butch. I know what I like, but my libido is adaptable to situations.

*

The collapse of Dateline Asia worked out well for me if not for my unfortunate partners. Without my then realizing it, the downfall set me on the road to letting go of the ego-tripping. Although still acting the hotshot journalist and avoiding Buddhism, I began reciting poetry as well as writing it. At a café called Our Place SW7. A café I'd even written about for the *Bangkok Post* well before starting the features service. This in a column describing a Beat poetry reading I distinctly recall attending with Irwin Block.

Irwin was the *Bangkok Post*'s Laos correspondent. He was also a Canadian Jew faced with a tricky dilemma when thinking to take a Laotian wife.

SIDESTREET

EDWARD WOODS

RECLINING ON THE BIG SOFA down at Our Place SW7 the other week, occasionally sipping some black coffee and listening to a reading from the poetry of Lawrence Ferlinghetti: stark recollections of the Beat Generation, the mid-sixties heyday of Allen Ginsberg, Jack Kerouac. Pre-hippy era when the idea was not to opt out but to seek, to know the world and search the soul, really looking for answers.

Kerouac, asked to define Beat, said: "Beatific, or maybe Beatitude. We're looking for God, demanding that He show His face." He never did, and the alienation of youth evolved onto a new plateau, neither up nor down, but sideways within another dimension. Asocial, apolitical, a-everything.

Ferlinghetti opened the City Lights Bookshop in San Francisco, then began publishing some of the most identifying literature of the period, his own and others'. "Howl" burst upon the world as the first issue of the Pocket Poet Series and even the intellectuals stood in momentary horror of its reviling, unconforming author. But that long, ear-splitting, poetic denunciation of the inhumanity of civilisation is good for today, as well, and Ginsberg managed to carry his Hindu/Buddhist oriented mind into the age of tranquility, into prophetic gurus, The Beatles and "Let It Be."

Ginsberg is with us and fully alive, but Jack Kerouac was no longer read at the time of his death. The franticism of his mad rushing across the country, breaking mental barriers and taxing his physical strength, was quietly, almost unnoticeably supplanted by a new breed of wanderer. His trip had no message for Haight-Ashbury and the cross-continental hippy. Quietude was less traumatic than beatitude, and the pungent odour of pot replaced tall shots of rot-gut booze drunk in the sleazy gin-mills of Denver's Larimer Street. Dean Moriarity and his jalopies died a silent death in the bookstalls.

Ferlinghetti, too, is very dated, nearly insulated. The 1950's are impregnated in every taut, supercharged line of his verse. Hearing the words, you can also see Christianity being hauled naked from its plastic superstructure and brought back through the centuries to face the simplicity of the catacombs. Stately princes of the Church are humiliated in the gutters of New York's Christie Street, before the ramshackle doors of the Catholic Worker Movement's home for the indigent. Christ Himself is exposed, … filement, re-deified.

But the spirituality of the Beat generation's revolt was also its downfall; though shouting obscenities at society's rank-and-file, they continued to nurture a fragmented germ of hope. In the end, of course, that hope failed and their successors simply walked off into the mountains and have yet to look back.

Lying there, listening with clenched eyeballs to the truth and shrill beauty Ferlinghetti's "Coney Island of the Mind," the memories were clear enough: scruffy poets and painters with virile minds huddled around hours-old cups of coffee at Rienzi's on MacDougal Street in Greenwich Village, or at the Cafe Bizarre or the Cock 'n' Bull. Genet's "The Balcony" is playing to off-Broadway passers-by and the uncertainties of Beckett cause mournful nods of acknowledgement, because in a sense we are all Waiting for Godot.

The Village Gate has just opened and is very cheap, very good, and Kenneth Rexroth has begun to read poetry to a jazz background at the newly opened Five Spot in the Village East: unhappy bohemians have migrated across town before the onslaught of tourists and gaudy, high-rent apartments near Washington Square.

Three thousand miles away, in the New World which California is becoming, Ginsberg, Kerouac, and Ferlinghetti hold forth in an auditorium overflowing with gallon-bottles of red wine. The kindly poet-doctor, William Carlos Williams, smiles and consents to be published at the City Lights. From New York, a newcomer, the unhip Marie Ponsot, sends tight, finely inscribed lyrics; she does this because she, too is deeply religious, though she scorned the sometimes coarse style of the Beats. Now her slim volume, "True Minds," survives only in quaint copies at the English Bookstore in Paris.

Ferlinghetti's words ring across the room, piercing a thick cloud of smoke:

"Him just hang there
   on His Tree
         looking real Petered out
   and real cool
         and also
according to a round-up
      of the late world news
from the usual unreliable sources
         real dead."
   They called for God and He never answered. Today, at least, we've learned to save our breath.

"It'll be bad enough telling my parents I'm marrying a shiksa," he lamented. "But a shvartzeh shiksa? Talk of oy veh!"

Reporting for ABC News helped hone my craft as a poet in a most unexpected way. All news items had to be in 35-second spots. That's not many words for a complete news story, but it can be done. It had to be done if I wanted to get paid! From that I learned the value of employing modifiers selectively. And as far as possible creating images by letting verbs move nouns. It's a powerful poetic tool.

Then came the coup de foudre. Or to put it more cogently, the 'coups de sublime.' The first was thanks to a joint I smoked one evening that whisked me away to a psychedelic realm where marijuana had never before taken me. I'd had in mind to head for the bars, but didn't even make it out of my suite. And only from the bedroom to switch off the stereo (Roland Kirk at his weirdest!) and then crawl back. At the time it seemed like a horribly bad trip. Enough for me to contemplate slitting my throat. Assuming I could find a razor! In fact it proved to be the very opposite of bad. As per McDonald's Corollary to Murphy's Law, that in any set of circumstances the proper course of action is always determined by subsequent events. My 'I-sense' needed that tortuous odyssey. Needed to experience existing as the tiniest and least significant micro-particle imaginable. Less than nothing and all there was. Alone and helpless in the unbearable vastness of infinite time and space. And yet unable to let go of 'being me.' This in order to prepare my psyche for the next step, an altogether different voyage of exploration.

Had Tennessee Williams ever been where I went to on that night? A night that, until I finally dove into a deep sleep, was like living through thousands of terrifying lifetimes that wouldn't stop recurring. (Lying belly down, I was gripping the mattress with both hands, so as not to fly off to a more frightening unknown.) I do not for a moment doubt that he had. And without the aid of marijuana to take him there.

I have a high tolerance for drugs and alcohol. As a kid I could drink most adults under the table without getting drunk. I know how to drink. Slowly, and never on an empty stomach. While with drugs, when I first tried any kind nothing happened. So it was with those joints I smoked in Hong Kong. Good grass, but nada. Ages later, in Amsterdam, I had to work damn hard to get a coke habit. Or as I prefer to call it, 'my eleven-year love affair with the white lady.' An affair I in no way regret. We did good things together. But both knew by the early 1990s that it was time to call it quits.

Harry Rolnick gave me my first acid trip. I saw colors and recall a wall seeming to melt, but that was it. There was a book on one of his shelves entitled *LSD and God*. 'What the fuck's that all about?,' I wondered. My next trip answered the question, in spades. It was with Daryl Cantor, post-Dateline Asia. Some chick had given him two tabs and said take half. What half? We took one each and then whoosh! Into the white light, becoming the white light, seeing God and being God. A no-holds-barred satori number. On and on it went, and it was glorious. Daryl and I were at one with ourselves and each other. (Eddie the prick had been given his walking papers and a new Eddie was hatching.) We were the universe: neither of us was an 'I' that could be separate from it or anything else. The mark all this made on my consciousness is still there. Along with the mind-altering impressions left by the hundred-odd trips I subsequently took (acid, psilocybin, mescaline), they bring me ever closer to an understanding of absolute reality. Nor have I ever had a bad trip.

Then we started coming down and got to feeling hungry. But were too stoned to order from room service. I rang Harry's suite and asked him to help us out. The Camelot fiasco aside, we'd remained pals. (It was an incident that occurred after I'd departed Bangkok, a nasty altercation between him and Carl, that put paid to our friendship.) When Harry walked in, Daryl and I were lying on the floor listening to the Beatles. Harry ordered hamburgers for us and left, returning a few minutes later carrying an LP. He took ours off the turntable and put his on. It was Bach's *St. Matthew Passion.*

"Got it?" I heard him say, seconds before I flew back into the white light, embraced by the mystical magic of Johann Sebastian.

*

Things were moving at a rapid-fire pace. Though

without my yet knowing it, the end was drawing nigh. I kept on reporting for ABC and doing my other radio gigs. And writing for the *Nation Review* in Melbourne and *Insight* magazine in Hong Kong. I may have 'seen the light' (or at least got a good glimpse), but I was still hell-bent on making my name as a journalist. One story I did turn down was when Dr. Henn offered to provide me with a map of all the heroin labs in Thailand. Dear Dr. Henn, who throughout his long multi-faceted life (he died at age 96) had his fingers in more pies than anyone could hope to shake a stick at. It was a sincere offer, intended to further my career and fulfill his own DEA (Drug Enforcement Agency) agenda. Yes, well, let others go for the heroics and risk getting killed. I draw the line at putting my body in harm's way. It's the temple I live in, I want to keep it intact.

My residence permit came directly from General Prapas Charusathian. Prapas (pronounced Pra-pat) was deputy prime minister, commander-in-chief of the Royal Thai Army, and de facto strongman in the government nominally headed by Field Marshal Thanom Kittikachorn. He was also the uncle of a lady who was head-over-heels in love with me, Miss Ubol (U-bon), director of the public relations department that controlled Radio Thailand. She tried every possible ploy to get into my bed. And once even made it as far as my bed! By insisting that I invite her to where I lived. There was no way I could refuse. She was my radio boss, and an invaluable link to the most powerful man in the country. Besides which, I liked her as a person. But nothing more. So I wasn't entirely lying when I told her flat out that I couldn't have sex with her.

"Why not? Don't you find me attractive?"

I didn't, absolutely not. But decided that in this instance lying was the better part of valor.

"I'm homosexual, Miss Ubol. I can't do it with women. I hope you won't hold that against me."

"Oh, you poor boy," she said. "No, I won't. But I do feel sorry for you. Here, have a hug. If you ever change your mind, you know where I am."

Apart from getting me my residence permit, Miss Ubol arranged for me to be the first foreign journalist to interview her uncle in ten years. We spoke for well over an hour. With two of his aides, who stood at semi-relaxed attention near the door, fidgeting nervously through most of it, as though they'd never seen the general in such a garrulous mood. And so jovial. Withal, I detected a sinister side to his overall demeanor that suggested he could shoot you dead without blinking and not stop smiling. He was also big on practical jokes.

"I keep crocodiles," he told me. "One day I sent two of them down the canal to where Dawee lives. He was most upset," Prapas continued, roaring with laughter.

The good general was referring to his military colleague Air Chief Marshall Dawee Chullasap (Tha-wi Chun-lasap).

The interview done and dusted, Prapas ordered that photographs be taken. Me and him side-by-side, each with an arm on the other's shoulder and saying cheese for the camera. The *farang* reporter and his rapscallion ruler buddy. I think *Insight* used one (they'd commissioned the piece). If only I could see them now. And you too, dear reader.

I wasn't much fussed when on November 17th 1971 Prapas and Thanom bizarrely staged a coup against their own government. And quick like bunnies reinstalled themselves in the same positions they already held, and more. The purpose being to cement military rule by abrogating the 1968 Constitution, declaring martial law, banning political parties, dissolving the partially-elected parliament and replacing it with a wholly-appointed unicameral legislative assembly; and then running the Kingdom through a National Executive Council, which they of course dominated. Together with Thanom's son, Colonel Narong Kittikachorn (who was married to Prapas' daughter!), the regime was popularly known as that of the Three Tyrants. How right *Bangkok Post* editor Nick was in saying, when he organized that *New York Times* gig for me: "Now you'll get an up-close look at the Machiavellian world of Thai politics."

Thailand has a long history of coups. Some bloody, others not. This coup was bloodless. There were tanks on the streets, but mainly for show. The soldiers manning them didn't bother anyone. And the gatherings at the Executive Council's press center (yes, next to the *wat* where the Dalai Lama was holding court and dispensing *darshan*) usually had their fair share of interesting characters mingling about. It was there I got to know General Kris (Krit) Srivara. And to Kris' dismay the Russian cultural attaché. Whom I took to visiting at the Russian embassy and once in his home. Every time getting photographed by the police when entering and leaving.

The coup was one thing. Life went on. The public execution a grisly something else again. Two prime pillars of the Thanom and Prapas government were anti-communism and law & order. An opportunity arose to drive the law & order point home when some poor bumpkin attempted to rob a US Army sergeant at gunpoint and it all went terribly wrong. The sergeant resisted and tried to snatch the guy's weapon, the bumpkin fired, and the sergeant ended up dead. The Council didn't think twice about ordering the man's summary execution. No pretense of a trial, just shoot the bastard. Out in the open. And make certain the spectacle gets publicized.

As soon as I got wind of what was happening, I phoned ABC in New York. They said go for it, never mind the cost, get receipts and send us the bill. I hired a taxi for the six-hour roundtrip drive plus waiting time. And told the cabman to step on the gas going. There was no need to rush, however. It turned out to be a long day in the boiling hot sun, milling with a few hundred spectators waiting patiently for the moment of deadly truth. Except for the journalists, the throng were there for an afternoon's entertainment. With snacks and drinks vendors on hand to make the waiting more comfortable. Throw in a couple of rides and you might would have thought the carnival was in town. Yet this wasn't a town. It was the barren grounds of a ramshackle wooden police lockup on stilts in the outback of southern Thailand near to the US Army base where a dumbass sergeant had foolishly gotten himself offed.

Everyone knew someone would die that day. Only the prisoner not. The cops had been instructed to stay stum, he'd find out soon enough; keep him well opiated, is all. The first he learned of it was when they brought him out, shortly before the firing squad arrived. The gaping crowd said it all. He looked on the verge of fainting. Two police officers held him steady in case he did. Then slowly walked him down the several-meters high rickety stairs. From there he was led to a mixed-bag assemblage of police, military, civilians, and one Buddhist monk. The charges and death sentence were read out. He was given a pen and told to sign at the bottom. A Thai reporter was also present. He asked the man how he felt. Someone I'd drafted for the task translated this for me. I could hardly believe my ears. 'What kind of a question is that?' I thought. But it was the answer that sent a peaceful shiver up my spine.

"I killed a man," he said ever so calmly. "I took a human life and deserve to die. I hope that in my next life I will be a better person."

The Buddhist monk recited a brief prayer. Still in handcuffs, yet his steps now less wobbly, the prisoner was escorted by the same two policemen past a five-man naval firing squad that was now in position and taken behind a large white canvas screen with black target-practice concentric circles on it. Once there he was tied to a wooden post, facing forward. And left alone to await his fate. Seeing the policemen leave, I stepped forward and took up my own position immediately behind the riflemen, a tape recorder dangling from my neck and running, a camera aimed and ready to shoot. A Pentax Spotmatic, the trustiest of single-lens reflex workhorses. The naval officer in charge shouted out the usual commands. "Ready." Weapons off shoulders and held pointing upwards. "Aim." They aimed. Four rifles had live ammo, one had blanks. With none of the sailors knowing who had what. I'd been speaking into my recorder this entire time, describing in agonizing detail what was taking place. The instant the aim command was given, and with my voice all but choking, I said: "And now you will hear...the sounds of death."

"Fire." *Bang, bang, bang, bang, bang!* Five times five shots in rapid fire, most of which hit close enough to the bull's-eye to ensure the transformation from living being to corpse. Or as the Elizabethan poet and condemned conspirator Chidiock Tichborne put it in the best known of his few surviving poems: "And now I live, and now my life is done." Food for a Tennessee Williams play? I doubt it. But Jean Genet maybe.

I slept sprawled out on the back seat of the cab for most of the ride back to Bangkok. As I was about to speed off to the telecommunications center to feed my story to ABC, the desk clerk called out saying I had a call. It was Carl.

"I heard it was a real bang-up affair down there," he chortled.

"Fuck you!," I said, and slammed the phone onto its cradle.

I had a special credit card for my news calls to ABC. I'd ring and say I was ready to feed. Then attach my tape machine by unscrewing the phone's mouthpiece cover and fastening the recorder's speaker cord to a metal bit inside with an alligator clip. And press Play. For this story I began with my usual 35-second spots (you had to do three, each one slightly different). After which I fed in everything I had, culminating in the *bang*s. They ran it big and nationwide, sent me a congratulatory telegram, and paid me extra. But that was for US airwaves consumption. I wanted it in print and on my side of the world. And I had these photos. I bided my time before writing it up. Once the piece was ready, I sent it and the photos to the *Nation Review*. They too ran it big. With the firing squad photo. And naturally bylined it Edward Woods. (I wasn't yet using Eddie for my writings.) It made my name, all right. Though not in the way I intended. By failing to use a pseudonym, I'd blindsided myself. And damn near got imprisoned for it.

What greenhorn me didn't yet know, is that all embassies have a section whose job it is to carefully scan every newspaper and other periodicals published in the country where they are posted, looking for stories and news items pertaining to the country their embassy is representing. These get clipped and regularly dispatched to the appropriate ministry. Which is how my *Nation Review* story inevitably got plunked on the desk of my good friend General Prapas. According to Miss Ubol, his first words after reading it were: "Is this our Edward?"

Prapas was more than angry, he was furious. And particularly incensed by my saying that this execution presented a clear example of Thailand's 'typical disregard for the value of human life.' Hindsight wants to tell me that was a bridge too far. Yeah, maybe. But despite the constant smiles, and an instinctive penchant for gentleness, something of that does course through the psychological veins of Thai males. An innate aggressiveness that even Buddhism is powerless to restrain. Plus there was my personal moral outrage at what these fuckers had done. Which was nothing compared to what they would later do.

Miss Ubol was the first to inform me what deep shit I was in. And hard on her heels Carl. Whatever doubts I may have harbored about him being a spy, those were now laid to rest. They both told me the same thing. My arrest was imminent and all borders—land, air, and sea—had been alerted to detain me should I try to leave the country. Worse still, as a resident I needed an exit permit. Without that, I'd get turned away before they even glanced at their files. Which was 50-50 whether they would if I had one. Yet how to get that?

"You have to help me," I said to Miss Ubol. "I'm certain you can fix it for me. And without your uncle knowing. Once I'm gone, I'm gone. They won't even think to look for a paper trail."

"Yes," she replied, "I can. But then I'll never see you again."

"And if you don't you'll have to come to Bang Kwang Prison to see me! I'll be there till the bloody cows come home, and you know it. Please, Miss Ubol," I pleaded. "You must."

"Do you promise to come back someday?"

"I promise," I said. "As soon as the coast is clear."

"Okay, I'll do it. But you better keep your word."

I had the funds to make a clean break. Eddy Rose's safely stashed purloined bread was more than sufficient to carry me for several months. And Carl was sitting pretty with the profitable remains of Dateline Asia. Armed with my partners' voting proxies (which I fast-talked them into giving me), by a few strokes of 'typewriter legerdemain' I'd already transferred that. Just as I would now arrange for Carl to take over my suite in the Trocadero, much to Harry Rolnick's intense displeasure.

"Where will you go?" Carl asked me.

"Bali. I've no idea what I'll find there. But it's bound to be a lot different than what I've been doing here. I need to lose myself."

I phoned Basuki Abdullah, requesting that he see me right away.

"Come," he said. "I'll be at home."

Basuki was a noted Indonesian painter, an erstwhile intimate of Sukarno, and from 1962 till 1974 Thailand's royal court artist. After I'd interviewed him for the *Bangkok Post* we'd become casual friends. He was big on throwing dinner parties, loved beautiful women, and constantly brimmed with *joie de vivre*. He also had important connections with Indonesian officialdom. And once insisted that if I ever felt to visit Indonesia I should call on him first.

"Here," he said, handing me the letter I'd watched him write and that was now in a sealed envelope. "It's to the Indonesian consul general. I'll phone and tell him you're on your way. He's there, I had reason to speak with him earlier."

"Yes," said the consul, all smiles. "Welcome. Basuki rang that you were coming. Any friend of Raden Basuki is a friend of mine."

After reading Basuki's letter, the consul wrote one of his own.

"Give this to the head of immigrations in Den Pasar. We're good friends. And he admires Basuki's work. All Indonesians do. Oh, and where's your passport? Right," he said while putting a stamp in it, "that's a visa for three months. When it's about to expire, my Den Pasar friend will give you a letter for the proper official in Jakarta. Then you'll be able to stay in Indonesia for as long as you like. A rare privilege. My country awaits you, sir."

I booked a flight to Den Pasar (Bali's small capital city) via Jakarta, but with an open-ended stopover in Singapore. Then sent a telegram to Kim saying when I'd arrive and to please meet me at the airport. Packing went quickly, even though I had way too much junk. Ninety-nine percent of which would be gone by the time I split Bali more than six months later. My books, record albums, stereo equipment and such I left behind for Carl.

"I trust you have your fingers crossed," I said to Carl and Jay as we three were taxi riding to the airport. And inconspicuously held my breath when presenting my travel documents at departures control.

"Ah, let's see....," the immigrations officer was saying more to himself than to me whilst leafing through my passport; although he did have to inspect the two added accordion pages to find what he was searching for, "you have a visa...and a, yes, residence permit...and okay, an exit permit. Everything is in order." He stamped one of the few empty spaces on the accordion and handed me the passport. "Enjoy your flight, sir." Whew! Now only to make it past the point of no return without the cockpit getting radioed to hightail it back to Bangkok. The moment we did I ordered a stiff drink. And silently thanked all gods great and small. The Singapore runway couldn't have looked more inviting had a red carpet been rolled out on it. Adios, Krung Thep.

The Three Tyrants' reign lasted until October 1973, when a massive student uprising led to their downfall. But not before many protestors were gunned down on orders from Thanom and Prapas. It was General Kris who halted the bloodshed by withdrawing the army from the streets. And reportedly yelling at Prapas, "Those are our children you are killing!" The tyrants went into exile in the United States. Exiles that were as short-lived as the democratic interlude that flowered during their absence. When Thanom returned to Thailand in 1976 and took robes as a novice monk, there were more violent protests and massacres, leading to yet another military coup. He died in Bangkok at age 92. Prapas only made it to 84.

Tennessee Williams liked Fidel Castro (he was introduced to him by Hemingway). But he most assuredly wouldn't have cottoned to Prapas. There are dictators and dictators. And jolly General Prapas was not among the nicest.

VIII

Kim was waiting in the arrival lounge. We hugged (of course we hugged). We kissed (of course we kissed). We drove from there by taxi to the apartment she'd borrowed from a friend. I remember windows and lots of light. I remember...tja. This part I'm sorely tempted to fictionalize. By way of reliving in my imagination all that went down between us. And allow you, dear reader, to delight in that with me. For sure we made love. And the lovemaking was good. Making love with Kim was always good, for her and for me. But this isn't a novel, it's a memoir of sorts. And while I'm not averse to embellishing, or even when necessary telling a little white lie, I am possessed of this ornery honest streak that forbids me to overstep that boundary. So here's what I do recall.

We both knew full well this was the last time

we'd see one another. Kim had asked to use her friend's flat so we could be alone. Wherever she'd moved to from Katong she was sharing, possibly with Amanda. (Kim was no longer on the game. Hooking had grown old for her. She was doing odd jobs. And painting.) She gave me an address. 73 Blanchard Drive, Singapore 9. Did I ever write to her there? I do not know. Those final days with Kim (two, three...?) are a blur. Ditto whether we had any contact later on. I had all this stuff. Big suitcases, with suits in them even. Huh? I was going to Bali, for chrissake! And sheaves of manuscripts, letters, all kinds of 'things.' I may have left my books and records behind, but the rest of my so-called life I was taking with me. Tennessee Williams took coals to Newcastle. I schlepped a shitload of crap to paradise.

And I had cameras. Three or four. Did I use any of them to take pictures of Kim? Methinks not. I was too self-absorbed. Instead I gave her a faded photo of me when I was fifteen. Pretty-boy Eddie and two magnificent Dobermans, Marlene and Yvonne. Why? Had she seen it before and liked it? I hope so. Otherwise it was madness. And when it comes to mementos, hardly the same as Tennessee Williams giving me a necktie. Or me popping a ball of opium into William Burroughs' hand in Amsterdam. Kim, one of the greatest loves of my life, and that was the best I could do? And scarcely remember the closing act? Shame on you, Eddie Woods. Shame on you.

*

Three months in Den Pasar. The Adi Yasar Hotel. One of the back courtyard rooms where only a handful of favored guests were accommodated, and where Prince Adi himself had his more lavish quarters. Then three months in Kuta. Dwelling comfortably in a grass hut that was less than a hop, skip, and a jump from the beach. Beach where one could behold the most astonishing sunsets on earth. When the roads weren't yet paved, and there was no electricity, and Japanese motorcycles were only beginning to tarnish Kuta's splendor. And where my mind got totally blown with awakenings day after day. And where in time I became variously known as Durian Ed and Mushroom Ed.

"What do you write on that typewriter anyway?" this New York dude asked in a cool-ass offhand way. We were sitting at the same table outside Janine's juice bar. Janine who'd started her career selling fruit from a basket on her head and then went on to own a neon-lit disco that got demolished in the Bali bombings of 2002. He'd observed me doing that from the road, tap-tap-tapping away at my all-metal Hermes Baby. I was on the porch of a place I'd rented for a week before moving to the grass hut.

"Oh, mostly letters," I replied defensively. And then thought: 'Yeah, he's right. Fuck words. No words necessary in the here and now. Off with their heads!' And so I burned everything. And what I didn't burn gave away or sold. Or traded, as with my shirts and ties and tailor-made suits for a set of gamelan drums.

(Drums I shipped to Eddy Rose, thinking he'd like them. But when I was passing though Munich in 1973 discovered to my horror that rather than serving as office ornaments they were used as stands for fruit bowls and heavy ashtrays, thereby badly warping the drumheads.) Got rid of everything but my travelers checks. 'Let's not be stupid about this,' I had the good sense to further think. Supreme relief. Free at last from attachments. And even more free once I'd narrowed my few remaining possessions down to what would fit into a small shoulder bag. Which, along with the checks and a blanket shawl and a rollup straw mat, was all I had with me when I got to Ceylon. And after traipsing around the emerald isle for three months, seeking enlightenment!, eventually landed at the Theravada Buddhist Island Hermitage.

"Can you type?" the abbot inquired of me one day.

I'd not told him anything about myself. To him I was simply a blank-sheet lay devotee who'd come to the hermitage asking to take Buddhist refuge. Or so I thought.

"Yes," I replied.

"Well, if I bring you this old typewriter I have and some paper, will you type up a few handwritten letters for me?"

"Certainly," I said. "But please don't you lug that across the island. I'll come to your *kuti* [Pali term for a small, usually one-room abode] and collect it."

Along with the typing machine and a stack of paper, the Mahathera [great elder] gave me a single letter that it took me maybe 10 minutes to type. I brought it to him and asked for the other letters.

"In time," he said.

Back in my *kuti*, I set the typewriter on the floor and the paper on top of it. Over the following weeks no more letters came. Nor did I mention them. Then of an early evening, whilst seated at my little table watching two geckos scurrying about, a stream of words that had the ring of a poem intruded on my solitude. They were so compelling that I couldn't resist hauling the typer off the floor and committing them to paper. One poem, two poems, three poems, more. Wow. When suddenly feeling a presence, I turned my head. Only to see the Mahathera standing on the other side of the screen door, gazing at me kindly. And the instant I espied him, walking away. It wasn't rocket science figuring out what had gone down here. The fucker had tricked me. Tricked me into doing what I was meant to do. Write!

Years later in Amsterdam I became friends with a lady who was in Bali the same time as I. Although we'd not encountered one another then, she did know that New Yorker who'd casually asked what I wrote on my typewriter.

"He's a writer," Meredith told me. "Obviously he was wondering if you were, too."

Here's the first of those poems I wrote thanks to the kick-in-the-ass wakeup call I got from the Venerable Nyanaloka Mahathera:

in the soft air above the palms
all manner of birds fly free,

117

through the tangled brake of the jungle island
the iguana silently stalks its prey,
each night on my window screen
two geckos chirp
and feast on fluttering moths.

never despair of love,
its voice rings clear with the light of dawn
and the sounds of the setting sun.

*

There are only two people I know for definite that I exchanged correspondence with during my stay in Bali, Harry and Carl. Harry wrote saying Carl had called the cops on him. I'd told Carl that when Harry returned from wherever he'd gone on holiday, to give him two large vases I'd said Harry could have. But Carl thought 'Fuck Harry' and didn't. So Harry slipped into what was now Carl's suite while a maid was cleaning it and took the vases. The cops charged Harry with theft, meaning he had to pay a bribe. And, Carl got to keep the vases! When I fired off a sharply-worded missive to Carl upbraiding him for what he'd done, he wrote back saying: "As you're well aware, in my book cop is **not** spelt PIG!" I did see Carl twice again, in Europe. First a brief encounter, arranged by Eddy Rose, in Munich's main train station. And later still in Amsterdam, at the office where I was editing the early issues of *Ins & Outs* magazine. The poet Ira Cohen was on hand, and he and Carl

Nyanaloka Mahathera,
abbot of The Island Hermitage in Ceylon.

got into a most lively conversation. Carl was with a young hippie wife who you just knew he was gonna divorce any minute. They said their goodbyes, we all shook hands, and Carl and I lost touch. So it goes. My friend the spy.

Bali and Ceylon were about getting my head together, not staying in touch with people. Gore Vidal asked me to, but I didn't. I doubt Bob Hope cared one way or another. Or Morey Amsterdam, et al. I was 'celebrity numb' by then. Bali, as you already know, culminated in the great renunciation fire. And oh what a pyre it was! Witnessed by many. A festive celebration of Eddie's past going up in smoke. I've often been asked if I regret having done that. No, I do not. It was necessary. It was the right move at the time. Sure, there are a few manuscripts 'n such that I wouldn't mind still having. But hey, if only seven of Aeschylus' plays survived (it's reckoned he composed something like 70!), who am I to complain! It's what I've done since and am doing now that matters.

*

Bangkok, Spring 1976. Strolling down Surawong Road with my girlfriend Jane. (Jane Harvey. We met in London in 1973, and were an intimate couple for eight years. We traveled extensively, mainly in South Asia; and on two separate occasions lived and worked in Iran. We started Ins & Outs Press together. We were also married for a spell. To this day Jane is still my very best and closest friend in the world.) Jane and I had gone to Kathmandu from Calcutta. After a month, Jane went on ahead to Thailand, leaving me to dive into the tantric mysteries of the Hindu goddess Maha Kali.

"This apartment [we'd rented one] is big enough for two people," she said. "You and Kali have fun."

We did. Even while I was getting sexually involved with a young German girl, Christina. Some weeks later, she and I flew to Bangkok. Jane was at the airport, checking on her next day's flight back to Nepal. No need for that now. Instead, the three of us shared a room at the Atlanta until Christina caught a plane home. She lived in the Ruhr valley. Jane and I were alone again.

"Ed Woods!" a voice calls out.

It was John Sipper. We clasped hands, I introduced him to Jane, I asked after Lance Woodruff and Irwin Block. Irwin had left Thailand, and Lance was 'speaking more slowly.'

"My wife says you owe us money," John said.

"I suppose I do," I replied. "Please say hello to her for me."

In Bangkok, before I arrived, Jane looked up Harry Rolnick, who readily invited her to lunch at the Trocadero. She told him about our travels, said I was in Kathmandu, she wasn't sure if I'd be coming, and was trying to decide whether to return. Harry was cordial, friendly, polite; and in no way intimated that he bore me any ill feelings. It therefore took me more than a little aback when (after Jane described her meeting to me) I rang Harry's suite from the hotel lobby, only to hear him say, "Unless you have money for me, I don't want to see you," and then slam the phone down.

Jane flew to England from Bangkok. I lingered for a few days before heading to the States via Hong Kong, Taiwan, and South Korea. It was my first visit in 12 years. [As of this writing there've only been two others, in 1980 and 1999.] I hung out for two months in San Francisco (I'd not seen the West Coast before that); hitchhiked through the Southwest, Deep South, up the eastern seaboard to Philadelphia, and on to New York by train. At long last I had circumnavigated the globe! Then I was in London, and reunited with Jane.

EPILOGUE

I've often been urged to write about my time with Tennessee. And while I didn't mind telling the stories privately, my answer to publishing them was always no. All the more so if it were in an article for some big-bucks paying mainstream publication. I considered it disrespectful, and in this case toward someone for whom I have a great deal of respect. Also frightfully transparent, trading on a famous person's name.

"But the guy's dead, Eddie," the urgers would say. "He'll never know the difference. Besides, you need the money, right?"

"I'll know," I'd reply. "And that's what counts."

Plus there was something else. Tom asked me not to. On our last day together, when he gave me the tie.

"May I write about you?" I asked.

"Oh no, baby, please don't," he said. "We know one another too well."

And he'd had unhappy experiences with people writing about him, referring to some of those as "brutal." Mohamed Choukri's Tangier journal was a notable exception, to which Tennessee contributed a 65-word note, thanking both the author and his translator Paul Bowles for the book's 'discreet and gently humorous tone.'

Then in late 2011, Theo Green wrote asking if I'd be up to writing a book about my times in Thailand or Persia in the 1970s. After mulling it over, I emailed back: "You're on, Theo. If you're into it, I'll give you *Tennessee Williams in Bangkok*. Which will also be the story I've long wanted to tell, about my drag-queen prostitute lover Kim."

And I have wanted that. Wanted it achingly. Wanted it for its own sake. Wanted it as a way of making amends to Kim for letting her vanish from my reality. And wanted it because Philip Wagner told me I must write it. Told me in San Francisco in 1976. Philip, whom Jane and I knew from Tehran and again in Kabul. Philip who upon hearing my tales of Kim said: "If Jack Kerouac could write a book about that black chick he had a brief romance with, then Kim deserves at least as much."

Jack's book is a novella, *The Subterraneans*. In it the girl's name is Mardou Fox. In real life she was Arlene Lee. (I briefly met Arlene in San Francisco in 1980, at a poetry reading.) Fine that Henry Miller penned a preface for it, but I never liked the book. As Kenneth Rexroth says in his review, two things Kerouac had no understanding of were jazz and negroes. He didn't understand women, either. Hell, he didn't understand himself half the time. Then again, how many of us do understand ourselves? A lot of what Jack wrote is good. He made a seminal impact on American literature. But some of his stuff is crap. *The Subterraneans* is in that category.

So with Philip's insistence firmly in mind, and my love for Kim still pulling at my heartstrings, and my respect for Tennessee as a man and a writer now stronger than ever (and feeling absolutely certain that at this stage of the game Tom would not at all mind), I set to work writing this book. I'm not quite finished, but will be soon. For me it has been a thoroughly delightful endeavor. I only wish Tennessee could read it. And Kim.

*

Some writers require biographers, others don't. Harold Norse, for instance, doesn't. His *Memoirs of a Bastard Angel* provides all the relevant inside poop on Harold, told in a free-wheeling style no one else could approximate. The same holds true of Tennessee for the first 60 years of his life. *Memoirs* portrays the definitive TW. Despite that, there have been several Williams bios of varying quality. One of those is *My Friend Tom*. Yeah, well, as Jimmy Durante amusingly put it: "Everybody wants ta get inta the act." Thing is, Tennessee Williams live is a hard act to follow. Among the titillating morsels his book reveals is that when it came to fucking, Tom did the penetrating. Btw, my first copy was a hardbound pirate edition I purchased in Taiwan!

Tom's younger brother Dakin also jumped on the bio bandwagon. Mere months after Tom's death, he rushed *Tennessee Williams: An Intimate Biography* into print. Co-written with Shepherd Mead, author of the bestselling satire *How to Succeed in Business Without Really Trying*, it has been generally regarded as at best opportunistic. This was, after all, the same Dakin who in 1969 had Tom committed to the psych ward of Barnes Hospital in St. Louis. A move which arguably may have saved the playwright's life, but hardly brought the siblings closer. Tennessee cut Dakin out of his will and bequeathed ten million dollars to the University of the South, a small liberal arts college in Sewanee, Tennessee. The real kicker came when Dakin published a new edition entitled *My Brother's Keeper: The Life and Murder of Tennessee Williams*. Tom murdered? What utter hogwash! When I read about how he died (in New York's Elysee Hotel), I instantly pictured him frantically trying to get that bottle cap off with his teeth and then choking on it. Tennessee Williams and Harold Norse, my two favorite hypochondriacs. The obsession kept Harold alive till nearly age 93. Tom it did in shortly before he turned 72.

Dakin had his post-mortem revenge. And not just with his absurd conspiracy-theory book. Against Tom's express wishes to be buried at sea near to where his poetic hero Hart Crane jumped to his death in the Gulf of Mexico, loving brother Dakin saw to it that Tom got interred in Calvary Cemetery in St. Louis, Missouri. The bio was the final straw. But what the fuck, a guy's got to make a buck, or? Or does he!

I find it interesting that I knew Tennessee long before I'd even heard of Harold Norse. But in time became close friends with Harold for the better part of three decades. While Harold and Tenn (which is what Harold called Tom) were very close from early on in both their writing lives. There are numerous references to Tom, and many lively descriptions of their interactions, in Harold's autobiography. I feel ever so privileged to have known both of them.

I said at the start that my story begins around where Tennessee's *Memoirs* more or less ends. And it certainly does where reflections on things past are concerned. He devotes no more than a single page to his sojourn in Thailand, and concludes that by saying: "The rest of my stay in Bangkok was a dream which I hope to have again someday. I wish that I had space here to extol its exotic delights!....All that was five years ago and now I am looking for another good excuse to return to Bangkok: perhaps I already have one, of a nonsurgical nature." That excuse never materialized. And even if it had, Tom wouldn't have found me there.

And Kim? I'm sure you'd like to know what became of her. Me too. But since I don't, I choose to think of her as alive. She lives in my heart. I loved her then, I love her still, and I always will.

"Everybody is nothing until you love them."
- Tennessee Williams in *The Rose Tattoo*

One Audience in Search of a Character

A dialogic contrivance in three scenes

by Edward Woods

INTRODUCTION: Part of this play was originally performed on Saturday evening, October 10th 1970, at the Oriental Hotel in Bangkok. The Main Personality was a noted American playwright born in 1911 in Columbus, Mississippi and known to the world at large as TENNESSEE WILLIAMS. The following scenes are loose representations of actual events. All characters are real enough. Any failure by them to accurately portray their true selves is the sole responsibility of the author. Who, by the grace of fortunate circumstance, was in attendance from the first fade-in.

CHARACTERS IN THE PLAY

Tennessee Williams: Sporting a moustache and closely-trimmed beard; casually attired in a flowery shirt, white-on-white Key West lounge jacket, and slacks.

A Close Friend: American.

A PR Girl: Pert lively Thai, projecting the steadiness that comes from continued nervous tension.

Ape, a Journalist: Chubby and rambunctious, somewhat of a stereotype Western newsman.

Mod, a Guest: Blond, pleasant stocky build; dressed perfectly in a neat ensemble created by a designer who was on a long trip with some very good acid. His trousers are white, his belt black and broad, and around his neck are several tiger claws.

Monday, a Writer: Tall, curly-headed, basically nervous type, sophisticated in his mannerisms and decisive in his gestures.

A Photographer: Thai male; wearing slacks, white shirt, and a conservative necktie; takes several photos during Scene One at the discretion of the Director.

A Dozen or So Reporters and Guests: Mixed male and female, mixed Western and Thai; conservative dress, not formal.

Three Foreign Correspondents: Attired as though they had changed rapidly, but not completely, from bush wear; carrying cameras and other equipment.

Three Life-Sized Marionettes: Dressed as waiters. These can be played by 'live persons,' but should be manipulated by strings with graceful awkwardness.

They stand at semi-attention and serve drinks at the Director's discretion; but will usually end up serving at inopportune moments, such as when someone is speaking or listening intently. Resumption of conversation frequently thwarts their efforts to reach the Main Personality's glass or ask him a question.

Twilight, a Writer: A tired and nervous Westerner, tall and too slender; conservatively attired in slacks, shirt, and tie.

The Commentator: Dressed casually in not-too-new sportswear, including a paisley ascot tucked under a pastel shirt, probably turquoise.

The Man with a Gun: Looks like an old-time city editor; long-sleeved white shirt, sleeve garters, loosened black knit tie, wrinkled trousers tightly belted under a moderate paunch.

Lyndon Baines Johnson: Texan.

A Girl: English.

Several Party Guests: Western and Thai, male and female.

A Waiter: Thai.

THE SET: The stage should be divided into three sets by Japanese screens. The center set is a hotel banquet room in which there is a long narrow table covered by a white cloth. Water glasses and round metal ashtrays are in sufficient supply. The chairs (Louis Quinze) are behind the table and facing downstage, but a few persons can be seated away from the table and facing toward it. A tape recorder is on the floor, and a modern mini-mike is placed at table center. Over the table hangs a sign reading: Mr. Tennessee Williams Meets The Press. The wallpaper, very elegant and with a constant fleur-de-lis pattern, is torn from the middle toward both extremities of the set and only a foot or so at either side can be seen. Instead, there is a multicolored, roughly painted representation of Streetcars, A Milk Train, One Cannibalistic Ritual in which a Homosexual is being Devoured, Southern Mansions and Shanties, A Cat-faced Woman on Tin Roof, City Lights, and Assorted Characters displaying various Emotions and degrees of Neuroses. (The Set Designer is free to improvise.)

The left-hand set is a cocktail party atmosphere: one small bar, stereo equipment, a few chairs and one settee, expensive-looking throw rugs (preferably white and fluffy), a small wooden coffee table.

These two sets share three-quarters of the stage. Set three, at the right, is a bare room on the wall of which is a huge office clock with a red second hand. There is also one typing table and a stool, a large and rather old Underwood typewriter, plus a full ream of copy paper on the table flap. The changeover from one set to another is accomplished by lighting alone; that is, sets not in use are blacked out. There is no curtain.

* * *

SCENE ONE: THE PRESS CONFERENCE

CENTER SET ONLY is gradually lighted with the participating characters already on stage: Mod, Monday, the Photographer, the Dozen or So Journalists and Guests and the Three Foreign Correspondents, the Marionettes, Twilight. They all stand around toward upstage with drinks in their hands and talk in muffled tones. Some smoke, as they will throughout the play. The Commentator also has a drink in his hand, and a cigarette in a black holder. He stands leisurely downstage and to the right. When the lighting is fully up: enter Tennessee Williams, The Close Friend, and the PR Girl from stage right.

WILLIAMS smiles, nods to the guests, shakes hands with a few to whom he's introduced by the PR Girl. The CLOSE FRIEND stands by inconspicuously.

After one or two minutes, the PR Girl leads WILLIAMS to the center chair (where he immediately sits) and then goes to a seat near the wall at the left. All but the Marionettes, the Commentator, and the Photographer seat themselves at random; except that Monday sits beside WILLIAMS, to his left; next comes Twilight, Close Friend, then Mod. The chatter subsides.

WILLIAMS (turning to a Marionette): May I have a dry martini? (He speaks slowly, with poised deliberation; his calm Southern accent is almost faint, and exceptionally gentle.)

[The Marionettes always say "Yes, sir," and

always go for drinks at Stage Right.]

MONDAY: Mr. Williams, why are you in Bangkok?

[Nearly everyone has a notepad, and most scribble intermittently.]

WILLIAMS (taking up the drink which a Marionette has placed in front of him): Why, I'm just on vacation. My oldest friend here (nodding toward CLOSE FRIEND, who remains inconspicuous-looking) is on sick leave from his university in California, where he's a professor. I simply thought it would be a good idea for me to also take a rest. Last time I was here—that's ten years back—I was entertained by Jim Thompson, the Silk King. A truly wonderful host. I understand he's lost now.

[Everyone nods as Williams slowly drinks his martini.]

COMMENTATOR (facing the audience): Jim Thompson, lost in the wilds. Maybe eaten by crocodiles. Or tucked away in a jungle shack, happy as hell he ain't coming back. (Turning toward Williams): Tell them about that one drink too many you took.

WILLIAMS (Putting down his drink and gazing with a smile ceiling-wards): Yes, I was drinking a bit much in those days. Passed out in his house. Ten years ago. Beautiful time I had. (Looking straight ahead): There seem to have been more canals here then.

EVERYBODY (in unison): Yes, there were, Mr. Williams. We filled them all in.

MONDAY: Filled them in for you, Mr. Williams. Are you happy about that?

WILLIAMS: Why, of course, I've always thought the people here were very charming. I'll probably stay here awhile this time, rent a house, travel around the country. (Looking about the room): It's time for me to relax. I've done most of the writing I'll ever do and I have been concentrating all my life on work. It's not worth it, not if you haven't learned to enjoy people.

MONDAY: And you weren't able to do that?

WILLIAMS: (When his mouth is closed, and mostly when he contemplates something, his lower jaw seems to jut out ever so slightly. Now he wraps both hands tightly around his martini, lowers his gaze, and answers in an almost choked voice): No. (The word floats out and dies quietly. He nods negatively.)

MONDAY: (Speaking softly. One almost has the impression he is a clergyman-cum-analyst): Can you now?

WILLIAMS (Same natural pose, but with less melancholy): Yes, I am finally learning. Before I was actually obsessed with my work and it was a dead-end street.

[From Offstage comes the loud crash of mirrors, glasses, a siren, howling children, and other noises and shrieks. The lights suddenly dim and bright colored lights flash across each other through the set. A woman calls out in a high, mocking voice: I AM MAGGIE THE CAT. A man answers: GODDAMN YOU ARE. Then calls: STELLA! STELLA! STELLA! There is a sudden crash, as of pots and pans being thrown down a metal staircase. Then silence and the normal set lighting resumes.]

WILLIAMS: A dead-end street.

COMMENTATOR (To the audience): In his own way, Tennessee Williams could always enjoy people, in spite of what he says. And this enjoyment was part of the very obsession which drove him into nearly seven years of morbid drinking and pill-swilling. Let me read you what he once wrote: "There is too much to say and not enough time to say it. Nor is there power enough…I have never for one moment doubted that there are people—millions!—to say things to. We come to each other gradually, but with love. It is the short reach of my arms that hinders, not the length and multiplicity of theirs. With love and honesty, the embrace is inevitable." (Turning towards WILLIAMS): Stand up and tell them what you've always wanted to do.

WILLIAMS (Slowly rises, stretches his arms wide and surveys the audience): I want to go on talking to you as freely and intimately about what we live and die for as if I knew you better than anyone else whom you know. (He lets his arms fall and slowly takes his seat. Everyone at the table looks downward.)

EVERYBODY (In unison softly and with deliberation): We will let you.

WILLIAMS: But I am not in fashion now. (He shakes away a Marionette who tries to give him another drink.)

MOD (With sincerity): I believe the world is waiting for you to become fashionable again.

WILLIAMS (Again embracing his nearly empty glass and holding it before him, both his elbows propped on the table; he raises one eyebrow, but has a hopeful expression on his face): I hope... (The phrase dangles awhile, then dies.)

MOD: The Western theater has undergone numerous changes during the past years. Have you been influenced much by the new trends?

WILLIAMS (Crossing his legs and cuddling himself, as he does occasionally throughout the scene): I was not much involved in anything during the sixties, other than too much deliquescence. I know almost nothing about what was going on in the theater, except for the one or two plays I was personally involved with. The wonder about them is that they were ever written.

GIRL REPORTER: Mr. Williams, are you a very lonely man?

WILLIAMS (With a short laugh and a broad smile): An English columnist once wrote about me that I'm the "loneliest man on God's green earth."

COMMENTATOR (Turning toward WILLIAMS): Maybe he was right. After all, aren't all writers lonely people? (WILLIAMS shrugs and finishes his drink.)

ANOTHER REPORTER: Do you go to see plays with nude actors and actresses?

COMMENTATOR (Looking at the audience): He does. (WILLIAMS nods in agreement.)

SAME REPORTER: What do you think of such plays?

WILLIAMS: Why not? Great theater may—no,

will—come out of it.

TWILIGHT: But that same English columnist you just spoke of quoted you as saying you didn't care for nudes. Did he misquote you?

WILLIAMS (Looking directly at Twilight): What was it someone once said about a foolish consistency?

EVERYBODY (In unison): Amen.

[Suddenly, from Stage Left, enter APE. He practically bounces onto the floor, throws his arms wide open, and grins.]

APE: Hi! Sorry I'm late. (Everyone looks at him. He sits, but not at the table, which is full.)

COMMENTATOR (Smiling at the audience): We really don't care.

[Everybody, except for WILLIAMS, nods negatively and together. At this moment, the CLOSE FRIEND leaves his seat, walks over to WILLIAMS, and begins whispering in the Main Personality's ear. Whilst he is so whispering, enter from Stage Left MAN WITH A GUN. The MAN, apparently unnoticed by those at the table (who begin to chat among themselves), crosses the stage and walks straight up to Twilight. He points his weapon, a long-barreled Magnum, at Twilight's head and wordlessly beckons him to come away. TWILIGHT stands without excusing himself, picks up his pad and cigarettes, and follows the MAN past the Japanese screen at Stage Right into the darkened third set; and on the way goes up to the COMMENTATOR (who appears bemused throughout this action) and hands him a sheet of paper. The lights flash on in Set Right (and remain on in the Center Set) as Twilight seats himself at the typewriter and rolls in a sheet of paper. The MAN taps on the table with his Magnum and points a finger at the clock when Twilight looks up. TWILIGHT begins to type feverishly. He continues in this way for the remainder of the scene.]

[CLOSE FRIEND has finished whispering now and exits at Stage Left.]

MOD: Have you ever tried LSD?

WILLIAMS: You cannot use LSD if you are neurotic. I wouldn't be able to take it.

REPORTER: Can you give us an idea of your political opinions?

WILLIAMS: I'm here for a holiday and certainly am not going to involve myself in political commentary.

EVERYBODY (In unison, softly, with feeling): Oyez, oyez.

MONDAY (to MOD): A very smart man. (MOD nods.)

COMMENTATOR: (To audience): A very wise man.

WILLIAMS: Besides, I'm a pacifist and my opinion is really worth nothing.

COMMENTATOR (To the audience): We should all hope that is not true.

MONDAY (Standing and talking to the commentator): But he's probably right.

COMMENTATOR (Still looking at the audience, first taking a sip of his drink): Of course.

APE (Dragging his chair to the table, where he

squeezes it in at the end): Listen, you've been telling people that you're not here for your health. Now let's get to the nitty-gritty of this. Haven't you come here to see a doctor for some (in a higher-pitched tone) mysterious disease?

WILLIAMS: No.

APE: Why are you going to the doctor then?

WILLIAMS (With admirable patience): I'm not.

APE: What's the doctor's name? What kind of operation are you going to have? Don't hold out on us, man!

[Enter LYNDON BAINES JOHNSON from Stage Left wearing cowboy clothes and a ten-gallon hat, and carrying a stuffed Beagle by the ears. He stops, still downstage and to the left of the table and faces the audience. He then throws the Beagle off the stage and yanks up his shirt, revealing a long red scar across his midriff and smiling broadly. Everyone at the table except the THAI REPORTERS AND GUESTS, MOD, and MONDAY, rush from their seats to look at the ex-President's belly.]

THOSE LOOKING AT THE BELLY (in unison): Oooooooooooooh!

[LYNDON BAINES JOHNSON drops his shirttail and exits, Stage Left, screaming: LINDA, LAY-DEE-BIRD. A voice from offstage cries: GODDAMN YOU, SHUT UP. STELLA, STELLA. The pots and pans crash again. Everyone returns to their places at the table.]

WILLIAMS: That was not, and never will be, me.

APE: When are you going for the operation?

COMMENTATOR (Walking over to WILLIAMS, reads from the paper handed him by TWILIGHT): Mr. Williams, aside from your fame and obvious financial success, would you say that you have been a success as a person?

WILLIAMS (With a very faint smile and looking exceptionally introspective): By comparison to what I expected, yes. I expected nothing.

EVERYBODY (In unison): Thank you very much.

WILLIAMS: Thank you. You are all very kind. Even you (nodding to APE, who grins).

[Everyone rises from the table. Many form into small groups and start chattering.]

[WILLIAMS walks halfway downstage, toward the right; but is stopped by several women holding out autograph pads. He signs a few, while most of the others present begin exiting toward Stage Left. When the Main Personality finishes signing the last pad and starts moving away, he is suddenly accosted by a leaping, smiling APE, who grabs his hand and nearly bellows at WILLIAMS.]

APE: Well, Tennessee, it was great meeting ya'. See ya' again sometime. And don't let them doctors cut too deep.

COMMENTATOR (To the audience): Last month he met Dick Nixon, whom he despises, personally and politically. He called him Mr. President. Eight years ago he met Jack Kennedy, whom he adored, personally and politically. He called him Mr. President.

[APE bounds off toward Stage Left, followed

by WILLIAMS and nearly everyone else still onstage. Last to leave are MOD, MONDAY and COMMENTATOR. When they finally enter the Left Set, the lighting there goes on but is not bright and is of mixed hue, and simultaneously goes off in the Center Set. And thus begins...]

SCENE TWO: THE PARTY

[Throughout this scene, the lighting remains on in the Right Set and TWILIGHT continues to type as the MAN WITH A GUN points his Magnum at him, periodically calling attention to the clock. At the Party are SEVERAL GUESTS; MOD, reclining on a throw rug, a pillow under his head; MONDAY, seated on the couch talking with one of the female guests; a WAITER, who simply stands by the bar, as everyone present already has a drink; and the ENGLISH GIRL, who is sitting on a chair, looking pleased with herself and speaking to no one. The COMMENTATOR sips his drink, down toward Stage Right, half facing the audience. The stereo is playing the theme from *Walk On The Wild Side*. People are sitting or standing at the discretion of the Director.]

MOD (Looking across to MONDAY): Where's Twilight?

MONDAY (Flicking his wrist): Gone to his Kafka's Doom, for all I know.

MOD (Almost sincerely): That's too bad.

MONDAY: It's no more than he deserves—or us, for that matter.

MOD: But I doubt that will ever happen to

Williams. They'll never lead him away like that.

MONDAY: Why the hell not? Just as Josef K. was eventually confronted by the insipid finiteness of his own existence, so did Tennessee Williams long ago realize how trapped he and all of us are within the limits of our very beings, our individual personalities.

MOD: But K never tried to break out of the dungeon, never let out a peep even.

COMMENTATOR: (Turning toward them both): And Tennessee Williams has not only tried, but very nearly succeeded. You saw him, you heard him, and watched his wistful visage. Yes, it was he who wrote that "personal lyricism is the outcry of prisoner to prisoner from the cell in solitary where each is confined for the duration of his life." But it was also he who (after years of giving himself an intellectual and emotional enema with pen and paper) finally came to understand that to have really begun one's life, the soul of a man must personally communicate with humanity.

MOD: Besides, even if such an achievement were not possible—and in all probability it's not—then at least this so-called enema has enabled the world to taste a little more beauty than it knew before and...

COMMENTATOR: ...and allow you to witness the resurrection of an all-too-human spirit.

MOD and MONDAY (In unison): Oyez, amen.

ENGLISH GIRL: (Perched forward on her chair): Who ARE you talking about?

EVERYONE, except MOD and MONDAY (In

unison): Tennessee Williams.

ENGLISH GIRL: Well, you're speaking as though you'd actually seen him.

COMMENTATOR (To the audience): He's not exactly a phantom, you know.

ENGLISH GIRL: (Anxiously): When did you meet him? Where?

MOD: Tonight, at a press conference.

MONDAY: Is there something so surprising about that?

ENGLISH GIRL: Well, he is rather, you know, larger than life.

MOD (With an honest, sincere smile): That's where you are so wrong. In fact, he is absolutely life-size. You know, a Mensch. A People.

ENGLISH GIRL: (With an almost horrified expression and placing her hand to her mouth): How frightening!

MOD and MONDAY (In unison): Wha-at?

ENGLISH GIRL: I mean, to think that REAL people are writing the books we read and plays we see. And sometimes even live by them!

MOD: I find it rather comforting.

MONDAY (Very clearly): And Amen to that.

FADE OUT

[With the lighting out in all but the Right Set, begin...]

SCENE THREE: THE EXECUTION

[TWILIGHT is still typing feverishly. After some 30 seconds, he stops and leans back on his stool.]

MAN WITH A GUN (Commandingly): C'mon, goddammit!

[The MAN points to the clock, which has just gone twelve. At that moment a bell buzzer rings jarringly from offstage.]

MAN WITH A GUN: Time's up, damn you!

TWILIGHT (Pulling the last sheet from the typewriter and placing it with the stack of completed copy): Finished. (He sighs and hands the manuscript to the MAN.)

[The MAN steadies the manuscript on top of his Magnum and begins to read. While he is reading, enter the COMMENTATOR from Stage Left (all of which is blacked out). The COMMENTATOR assumes his usual position, downstage right. He is again smoking through his cigarette holder.]

MAN WITH A GUN (After having scanned through the entire manuscript, but very quickly): Bastard!

[MAN WITH A GUN pulls the trigger. TWILIGHT lets out a short groan and falls to the floor. Exit MAN WITH A GUN at Stage Left. The COMMENTATOR merely shakes his head, as though to say: 'Why did you do it?' He means, of course: 'Why did TWILIGHT do it?' Enter TENNESSEE WILLIAMS from Stage Left, carrying a big wreath. He pauses before the body, then places the wreath on top of it.]

145

COMMENTATOR (Aside, to the audience): I hope he hasn't done that thinking the fool wrote well—because he didn't!

WILLIAMS (To the audience): No, because he wrote, dead-end street or not.

[Exit TENNESSEE WILLIAMS and the COMMENTATOR, Stage Left, while the lighting in the room changes from plain bulb white to multicolored flashes, as in Scene One. All the same noises begin again: Sirens, Screams, Pots and Pans, Wailing and STELLA! STELLA! LIN-DA! LAY-DEE-BIRD! And as the sounds eventually subside, FADE OUT.]

THE END

First published on the front page of the *Bangkok Post*'s Sunday Magazine, October 18th 1970. Vol. XXIV, No. 289.

INTRODUCTION. Part of this play was originally performed on Saturday evening, October 10 1970, when a press conference was held at the Oriental Hotel in Bangkok. The Main Personality at the conference was a noted American playwright born in Columbus, Missouri, in the year of Dylan Thomas (914) and known only by his real name of TENNESSEE WILLIAMS. The following 'scenes' are therefore loose representations of actual events. The characters are real and any future attempt to approximate their true selves is the sole responsibility of the writer who, by the grace of fortunate circumstance, was in attendance from the first fade in.

CHARACTERS IN THE PLAY

ONE
AUDIENCE
IN SEARCH
OF A
CHARACTER

A dialogic contrivance in three scenes
by EDWARD WOODS

Also Available from Inkblot Publications

brion gysin
LIVING WITH ISLAM

stephen davis
TO MARRAKECH BY AEROPLANE

stephen davis
WILLIAM BURROUGHS /
LOCAL STOP ON THE NOVA EXPRESS

michael spann
WILLIAM S. BURROUGHS'
UNFORGETTABLE CHARACTERS

***

all above titles $12 plus shipping.

available from:
aftermath books
42 forest street
providence, rhode island
02906
usa

www.aftermathbooks.com
orders@aftermathbooks.com

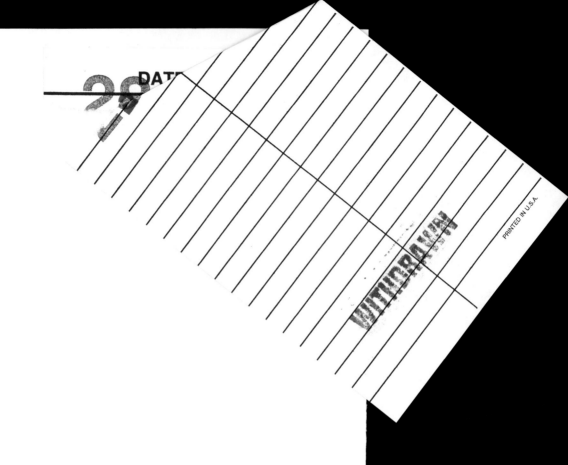

811
W894

Woods, Eddie,
1940-
Tennessee Williams
in Bangkok

CPSIA information can be obtained
Printed in the USA
LVOW13s1311150114

369524LV00005B/4/P